FAMINE

Famine Life at the Cork Union Workhouse

THE USE OF
Indian Meal as an article of Food.

Various Manners of using Indian Meal, as Human Food.

Suppawn, or Porridge, that is to say, boiling milk, or water, thickened with Indian Corn meal. Put into water, this is a breakfast, supper, or dinner for little children; put into milk, it is the same for grown people. In milk it is a good strong meal, sufficient for a man to work upon.

It takes about three pounds and a half of Indian Corn flour to make porridge for ten persons, less than half a pound of corn flour for a meal for one man, and a warm comfortable meal that fills and strengthens the stomach. Three pounds and a half of wheaten flour would make four pounds and a half of bread, but it would be dry bread, and bread alone; and not affording half the sustenance or comfort of the porridge.

Mush.—Put some water or milk into a pot and bring it to boil, then let the corn meal out of one hand gently into the milk or water, and keep stirring with the other, until you have got it into a pretty stiff state; after which let it stand ten minutes or a quarter of an hour, or less, or even only one minute, and then take it out and put it into a dish or bowl. This sort of half pudding half porridge you eat either hot or cold, with a little salt or without it. It is eaten without any liquid matter, but the general way is to have a basin of milk, and taking a lump of the mush you put it into the milk and eat the two together. Here is an excellent pudding, whether eaten with milk or without it; and where there is no milk, it is an excellent substitute for bread, whether you take it hot or cold. It is neither hard or lumpy when cold, but quite light and digestible for the most feeble stomachs. The Indian Corn flour is more wholesome than wheat flour in all its manners of cooking. It is a great convenience for the workman in the field that mush can be eaten cold. It is, in fact, moist bread, and habit soon makes it pleasanter than bread. It is a great thing for all classes of persons, but particularly for the labourer. He may have bread every day, and he may have it hot or cold; and there is more nutrition in it than you can get out of the same quantity of wheat flour. It is eaten at the best tables in America almost every day; some like it hot, some cold, some with milk, some to slice it down and eat it with meat; some like it best made with water, others with milk, but all like it in one way or another. Some put these cold slices again into the oven and eat them hot, or they might be heated on the griddle. It is believed in America that the Indian Corn, even used in this one single manner, does more, as food for man, than all the wheat that is grown in the country, though the flour from that wheat is acknowledged to be the best in the world.

The usual mode of making bread or cake of Indian meal, is to scald the meal in boiling water, and make it of a proper consistency of dough, and bake it on tins before the fire or on griddles half an inch thick; and at the South and West, it is made three quarters of an inch thick. It is Indian Meal, water, and salt, of a consistency to roll out on a tin board, or flatten out with the hands.

It is also made into gruel, or thicker into hasty pudding, by stirring the meal into hot water gradually until it is of a consistency of starch, or a very soft pudding, which hardens as it becomes cold.

It is eaten with butter, fat, salt, or sugar, or treacle, or any relish of salt meat or fish, OR ALONE.

It also makes an excellent cake, by mixing it with coarse flour, in the proportions of two-thirds of Indian meal, and one-third flour.

No mistake can be made in using the meal, as it *can be mixed with, or adapted to anything.*

To Make Excellent Bread without Yeast.—Scald about two handfuls of Indian meal, into which put a little salt, and as much cold water as will make it rather warmer than new milk; then stir in wheat flour, or oatmeal, till it is as thick as a family pudding, and set it down by the fire to rise. In about half an hour it generally grows thin; you may sprinkle a little fresh flour on the top, and mind to turn the pot round, that it may not bake to the side of it. In three or four hours, if you mind the above directions, it will rise and ferment as if you had set it with hop yeast; when it does, make it up in soft dough, flour a pan, put in your bread, set it before the fire, covered up, turn it round to make it equally warm, and in about half an hour it will be light enough to bake.

Hasty Pudding.—Boil water, a quart, three pints, or two quarts according to the size of the bowl of ..... stir it well and let it boil up thick; put in salt to suit your own taste, then stand over the kettle and .....

FAMINE IN CORK CITY
Famine Life at Cork Union Workhouse

MICHELLE O'MAHONY

MERCIER PRESS

MERCIER PRESS
Douglas Village, Cork
www.mercierpress.ie

Trade enquiries to COLUMBA MERCIER DISTRIBUTION,
55a Spruce Avenue, Stillorgan Industrial Park, Blackrock, Dublin

© Michelle O'Mahony, 2005

1 85635 455 5

10 9 8 7 6 5 4 3 2 1

*This publication has received support from the Heritage
Council under the 2005 Publications Grant Scheme*

DEDICATION
*For my husband and my parents,
thank you for all your support.*

*Mercier Press receives financial assistance from
the Arts Council/An Chomhairle Ealaíon*

*This book is sold subject to the condition that it shall not, by way of trade or other-
wise, be lent, resold, hired out or otherwise circulated without the publisher's prior
consent in any form of binding or cover other than that in which it is published and
without a similar condition being imposed on the subsequent purchaser.*

Printed in Ireland by ColourBooks

CONTENTS

Acknowledgments   7

Introduction   9

1   The Origins and Development of the Cork Union
      Workhouse, 1838–41   13

2   The Role of Cork Union Workhouse during the Famine   35

3   Inmate Health   65

4   The Children of the House   96

5   Institutional Culture   127

Concluding Thoughts   143

Appendices

1   Cork Poor Law Unions Pre-1850 and Post-1850   146
2   Questionnaire on the Epidemic Fever in Ireland (1848)   147
3   Assisted Emigration, November 1849 and May 1850   150
4   Emigration – Inter-Union, Inter-Country   151
5   List of Physicians and Surgeons in Cork City 1846   152
6   Irish Workhouses, *Cork Examiner*, 20 September, 1847   156
7   Thirteenth Report of the Commissioners of National
      Education in Ireland   158
8   Table showing the increase in the National Schools,
      and attendance figures   159
9   Report on Cholera by the Workhouse Physicians   160
10 Salary Accounts, June 1847 and December 1848   163

Notes   164
Bibliography   175
Index   185

ACKNOWLEDGEMENTS

This book covers many aspects of life within the workhouse during the famine years. It is the product of research undertaken for undergraduate and postgraduate theses at the department of history, University College Cork. To ascertain the famine experience it was necessary that I consulted diverse sources and institutions. The most important of these were the minutes of the Cork union board of guardians. For this I extend a great deal of gratitude to the staff and archivists, both past and present, Brian Magee and Patricia McCarthy of the Cork Archives Institute. Their assistance was invaluable in dealing with my many requests and queries. I especially thank Brian McGee for allowing me to reproduce images from the records.

My thanks to Kieran Burke, Cork City Library for his assistance over the years. I express my appreciation to Colman O'Mahony, author of *In the Shadows, Life in Cork 1750–1930*, for a copy of John Arnott's text on the condition of children in Cork union workhouse. This text was fundamental to assessing the impact of the famine on the position of children in the workhouse.

Many thanks are due also to Mary O'Doherty, archivist of the Mercer Library, Royal College of Surgeons in Ireland, for her assistance in tracing the medical officers of Cork workhouse and providing me with swift access to the medical journals and writings of the doctors of the famine period. A thank you also to Malachy Powell, for a copy of his paper, 'The Workhouses of Ireland', which was read to the graduates society of University College Dublin in 1964.

In assessing the extent of similarities between the Cork union workhouse and its English counterparts, sincere gratitude to the following: Stephen Penny, curator of the Salt Museum, Cheshire, England and Martin Collier, director of Gressenhall Workhouse Museum and Norfolk Rural Life Museum for their information which served to highlight the differences between the Irish and English workhouse. These differences and similarities were useful in helping to put the Irish famine experience into perspective.

For their encouragement, advice and support throughout my postgraduate years and for having greatly informed my knowledge of history, I especially thank Professor J. Lee and Marita Foster and all at the department of history, UCC. Mary Feehan and the staff of Mercier Press must be acknowledged for their enthusiastic support. Sincere thanks to Frank Daly, Ronan Daly Jermyn for his encouragement in helping turn a dream into reality. To those who read this book I thank you for your interest in commemorating the suffering of the famine victims within Cork workhouse.

In acknowledging those who have helped, guided and assisted me, I have realised that I owe a debt of gratitude to so many and for those not mentioned I thank you sincerely. Finally, no book can be completed without the support of family and friends who are always on hand to give advice and on occasion cast their eyes upon the manuscript. To my husband, Mervyn and my parents, Jerry and Marie, I thank you for your patience, support and words of wisdom.

INTRODUCTION

This book was born as result of research undertaken for under-graduate and postgraduate study. As the one hundred and sixtieth anniversary of the famine approaches it is notable that this is the first detailed survey of life within the confines of Cork union workhouse during 1845–50. *Famine in Cork City* seeks to examine the impact of the famine on life within the institution. In each page one is reminded of the horrific conditions and human suffer-ing experienced by the largely anonymous witnesses of the famine experience. Beyond the clerical notes of the officers during that time the events of those years remain vivid in the folk memory of Cork city and its people. Deprivations experienced by the desti-tute of the city remain as indescribable today as they did back then for those charged with the duty of providing relief for the city's destitute. The workhouse has since become a landmark for all Cork. It is notable that the saint most renowned with Cork has given his name to a hospital. St Finbarr's hospital now occupies the workhouse site and it is still as important and integral a building to the Cork community in providing relief today as it was back then.

The fragmentary records of Cork union workhouse show not only the functioning of the institution but also highlight the wider social context of the famine era. The functionaries of the union, though at times appearing dispassionate, perceived themselves as 'warriors on a great administrative crusade' which would raise the 'moral tone of the whole community'.[1] Constrained by their ideo-logy and bureaucratic practices, the officers of the union, no more than the populace at large, could not have foreseen the circum-stances whereby the starving masses 'besieged the Imperial Bakery demanding something to eat ... and were only with difficulty kept under control by the police'.[2]

Beginning with an examination of the application of the poor law in Ireland in 1839, this book studies the local effects of a national calamity. The workhouse was an integral component of the efficient functioning of the poor law in Ireland. It is therefore necessary to trace the development of Cork's workhouse from its very origin. Close study of the famine years clearly demonstrates the impact of the famine experience on the day to day running of the workhouse. The book explores the historical, social, medical and cultural aspects of the workhouse, together with its salient role as an institution of relief 'in guaranteeing the indigent Irishman from starvation'.[3] Following the establishment of the workhouse in 1839, problems of administration and organisation abounded. There was much difficulty in accounting for and accommodating a large pauper population and these issues were largely dealt with through strict disciplinary procedures. Such procedures and 'house rules' were necessary to preserve order. However on occasion such rules and bureaucracy took precedence over the physical well-being and mortality of inmates. To assess the impact of the famine on the mortality and wellbeing of inmates it is necessary to understand the statistical evidence. Such evidence has been compiled from the existing manuscript sources relating to the Cork union workhouse. 'Famine is like insanity, hard to define but glaring enough when recognised'.[4] Increased death tolls were the most obvious means of recognising that famine had arrived. For most of the famine years the level of inmates far exceeded the capacity of the house and statistical evidence shows how this led to certain problems. Even when sheds and extensions were added, inmate levels continued to spiral out of control. However it is notable that the guardians were resolute in attempting to administer relief to as many destitute persons as possible. Though restricted by the capacity of the house they tried to extend relief to as many as possible which often resulted in short terms of residency for paupers within the house.

Fragmentary registers reveal that the residency period of inmates varied from a single day to several weeks depending on their destitution. Though 'no board of guardians could conceivably relieve the destitute efficiently and economically' the Cork guardians managed to sustain and regulate an inmate population of 7,100 during August 1849.[5]

Studying the empirical evidence leads to a tangible sense of the cramped, overcrowded and, needless to say, deadly atmosphere which prevailed in Cork workhouse. With this in mind the issues of health and welfare of inmates and more specifically issues of nutrition and disease come to the fore. *Famine in Cork City* seeks to shed light on the physical conditions of inmates and the relevance of their environment to their actual wellbeing. The rising inmate population threatened the health of those within the walls of the workhouse. Increased numbers were in the main accompanied by an increased incidence of disease and in some instances the question arises – was the workhouse environment a malign influence within itself? In addressing this question and the issues of inmate health it is only fitting to examine the medical officers of the union together with the guardians' responses to the recommendations of such medical officers. Too often their recommendations were not implemented or only mildly implemented. At all times it is important to recognise that medicine was not what it is today and often miscalculations and speculation abounded concerning illness, treatment and avoidance of ill health. Stemming from the health aspects and the social makeup of the workhouse it is perhaps fitting that the missing generation of famine victims – innocent children – and their experience of workhouse life are not forgotten. Due to the segregation policies implemented in the house children were separated from the family unit. Smaller children were allowed in some instances to remain with their nursing mothers but not always. Separation coupled with the ongoing famine must have left a psychological impact on the workhouse children. Stunted physically and mentally, these children developed the appearance of old men and women.[6] Such descriptions written after the famine are a poignant reminder to the misery endured within the workhouse walls. The concluding element of this book describes the actual institutional culture of the workhouse and how it fulfilled many roles. It was an employer of sorts in terms of providing relief in return for work in the various departments. Spinning, carding and tailoring were among the 'mini' industries. It had a judicial culture of its own, often acting as judge and jury. Inmates' lifestyles were strictly regimented in accordance with the poor law regulations. Disciplinary procedures which were quite punitive were enforced with haste for those who transgressed house rules. It is worth revealing that the staff at the workhouse were not immune from breaking rules and receiving punishment, usually in the form of redundancy. What is more revealing is the fact that in a few instances staff sided with the inmates and were punished for attempting to improve their conditions. It also revealed that when faced with catastrophe the workhouse staff were as humane as they could be within the constraints of the poor law system.

The workhouse by its nature was a warehouse for the poor where efficient organisation was of the utmost importance. The poor law administrators of each workhouse irrespective of the famine conditions still had to balance their accounts and this has often led to unfair criticism. Perhaps the Cork workhouse officials did the best they could in the circumstances. The workhouse was a multi-faceted institution incorporating the roles of many institutions. In carrying out their duties, administrators sought to replicate the norms of life beyond the high walls of the workhouse. Issues of emigration, marriage and religion mirrored the beliefs of the age. These serve as a microcosm of the wider society.

Famine in Cork City seeks neither to vindicate the actions of the poor law administrators and guardians nor to engage in condemnation. Rather it seeks merely to present the evidence, commemorate the suffering and record the legacy of the famine experience at Cork union workhouse.

MICHELLE O'MAHONY

1

THE ORIGINS AND DEVELOPMENT OF CORK UNION
WORKHOUSE, 1838–41

> Cork is the second city in Ireland, and is distinguished for its fine
> harbour, derived its ancient names Corcach and Corcac-Bascoin,
> signifying in Irish language 'a marshy place' from its situation on the
> navigable river Lee. The earliest authentic account of its origin
> occurs in St Colgan's life of St Nessan, to whose preceptor, St Barr or
> Finbarr, is attributed the foundation of a cathedral church, to which,
> as the abode of that saint, such numbers of disciples resorted from all
> parts, that the desert in which it stood soon became the site of a
> considerable city.[1] The foundation of the See of Cork is generally
> ascribed to St Barr or St Finbarr, in the early part of the 7th century:
> his relics, which were enclosed in a silver shrine, were carried away
> from the cathedral in 1089, by Dermot, the son of Turlough O'Brian,
> when he pillaged Cork.[2]

Natives of and tourists to Cork city will be familiar with the name
of St Finbarr, the cathedral and the relevance of this saint to the
history and culture of the city. What is less familiar is that the hospital, called after Cork's patron saint, was during the famine years
the site of the Cork union workhouse and from its inception was
dedicated to providing relief to the poor of Cork city. Today, some
one hundred and sixty or so years after its construction it is still
providing relief, albeit of a different nature. Nonetheless this building is still as essential today as it was from its very construction. Its
history during the hungry years can be described as harrowing and
ghastly and it stands today as a structural reminder of the famine
in Cork city. To understand the importance of this building between 1845–50 it is essential to chart its very origin and the legislation that paved the way for its construction.

The workhouses of Ireland were established under the Poor
Law Act of 1838 and came to especial prominence during the

great famine. The workhouses were by no means a new concept. To understand the operation of the workhouse in the famine years it is necessary to be familiar with the workhouse concept and its very nature from its earliest origins under the poor law of 1601 to the Poor Law (Ireland) Act as was implemented in 1838. What follows is a discussion of the objectives of both the old and the new poor law. It specifically examines the legacy of the old poor-house and the development of the new poor law workhouse in Cork.

The primary difference between the old and the new poor law workhouse was that the new workhouses were more regulated and regimented than their earlier counterparts of the seventeenth and eighteenth centuries. The poor law of 1601 classified the poor into two groups, the deserving poor and the undeserving poor. The deserving poor were deemed to be those who were unable to work, for example the blind, the elderly and the disabled. Able-bodied unemployed were labelled the undeserving poor. Those unable to work received outdoor relief, usually in their homes either in the form of financial assistance or in kind. Those capable of work were provided with government subsidised work, i.e. indoor relief. Indoor relief was largely facilitated in specifically designed houses of industry. The Cork House of Industry was located near to the site now occupied by the South Infirmary hospital. Workhouses and houses of industry were long associated with poverty and deprivation, they were frequently referred to as poorhouses and workhouses.

The main objectives of the 1601 poor law were to establish a sense of local responsibility, to determine a reasonable amount of relief and to identify those people eligible for relief. It encouraged children to work and to serve apprenticeships. The poor law sought the suppression of vagrancy and to provide work as a means of welfare. The law makers at that time felt it was essential to the functioning of the 1601 poor law that there be included in the law a provision for the creation of a correctional facility for 'those who refused to work or spoilt work or went abroad living or begging idly'.[3] The general opinion amongst the earlier poor law officers was that the poor were a 'thriftless section of society to be feared, strictly controlled and punished where necessary.'[4]

It was not until 1735 that Cork Corporation petitioned parliament on the issue of the construction of a workhouse for the city. An act was passed sanctioning the establishment of the city's first workhouse for 'employing the poor, punishing the vagabonds and providing for and educating the foundling children.'[5] A board of governors was installed to administer the fledgling workhouse and it was funded through revenue collected from imports of coal and anthracite into the port of Cork, at the rate of one shilling per ton. The governors first met in May 1736, a site on the Watercourse Road was identified in 1737 and Cork's first workhouse was officially opened in April 1747.[6]

Although this workhouse was officially intended to be a combined workhouse and foundling hospital, in practice it served entirely as a foundling hospital. Subsequently, a house of industry was established in the city to provide the system of indoor relief.[7] It was located off Douglas Street, on the junction between South Terrace and Langford Row. Adjacent to the house of industry was an infirmary. These ambitions of the early administrators were largely irreconcilable; 'combining two objectives, punitive and ameliorative' whilst they achieved neither.[8] Thus poverty and destitution continued unabated without remedy.

In 1830 the House of Commons appointed a committee under Archbishop Whately of Dublin, to consider the case of the poorer classes in Ireland and to suggest remedial measures. Proposals included the extension of the existing practices of relief, assisted passage, reclamation of bogs and wastelands and the possible adoption of a poor law either along English or Scottish principles.

Consequently, from 1833 to 1836 a royal commission was set up under Lord Grey's government. It investigated the social and economic conditions of the poorer echelons of Irish society. The commission's report outlined the unfeasibility of operating the English workhouse system in Ireland since: 'our conviction is that the able-bodied in general and their families would endure any misery rather than make the workhouse their domicile.'[9] The commission's proposals would have required a level of state intervention that ran counter to the economic theories of the day which emphasised a system of laissez-faire.[10] It did, however, suggest the division of the country into relief districts, with local boards of guardians to dispense relief. Lord John Russell, leader of the House of Commons, acting upon the report, appointed Sir George Nicholls, an English poor law commissioner, to investigate the Irish situation further.

Between September and November 1836 Nicholls visited Cork, along with sixteen other towns, investigating the extent to which the Poor Law Amendment Act of 1834 could be implemented in Ireland. In his report Nicholls recommended transplanting the model of the new English poor law system to Ireland. Dismissing the findings of Whately's commission Nicholls perceived that, 'the Irish are easily governed and led, as in the workhouse they would be free from the influence of ardent spirits and other excitements, I anticipate no difficulty in establishing an efficient system of discipline and classification.'[11]

Ironically, a general famine was the only scenario with which, in his view, a proper poor law could not cope. Since 'the habits and intelligence and forethought of the people would improve with the increase of wealth and with the progress of education' the suggestion was dismissed.[12] Ironically, it was considered unlikely that a considerable proportion of the Irish poor would experience famine.

Acting on Nicholl's report the Whig government introduced the Poor Law (Ireland) Act in July 1838. It was modelled on the English poor law system. A central body of poor law commissioners was drawn from the commissioners of England and Wales who were then appointed to facilitate the introduction of the act into Ireland. They were vested with authority to appoint assistant commissioners to help them in their task. On 11 September 1838 four assistant commissioners arrived in Dublin.[13] The English assistant commissioners were Richard Earle, William J. Voules, W. H. T. Hawley and Edward Gulson. None of them had any experience of Ireland and were expected to rely upon their own experiences of the poor law in English and Welsh unions.

The country was divided into 130 'groups of parishes or unions' subdivided into electoral districts.[14] Unions were compactly designed with a market town at their centre (where the workhouse would be usually situated) and within a suggested radius of ten miles.[15] To facilitate geographical awareness, a map was issued to each commissioner with the market towns encircled.

Each union was administered by a board of guardians, responsible to the poor law commissioners in Dublin. These boards were composed of elected and *ex-officio* members; the *ex-officio* guardians were magistrates residing within the union and their number was not to exceed one-third of the elected members. Elections were held annually and all ratepayers would be entitled to vote but a multiple voting system allowed for extra votes for the larger ratepayers. All adult males paying rates of 10/- or more and landlords in receipt of an annual rent-roll of at least £10, would be eligible for election. Clergymen were excluded.[16] Levying a poor rate provided the finance for the Irish poor law system. The burden was to be shared between the landowner and the occupier. Each union erected a union workhouse financed from a levy on the ratepayers within the electoral districts, in addition to a loan advanced from a state or provincial bank. Relief was only to be administered within the workhouse and each electoral division was responsible for the financial support of its own poor. This however was problematical during the famine years as many of the country's poor travelled from the countryside to the cities and market towns in the hope of receiving relief and some unions faced increased financial burdens. The act also provided assisted passage for those willing to emigrate. Such assistance amounted to the value of one shilling in the pound of the poor rate. Again during the hungry years this idea of assisted passage was a further financial burden for many unions. Thus the economic aspects of each union played a central role both in the administration of the union and the workhouse.

This wide-scale introduction of the poor law was assisted by the provision of additional revenue generated from the £4 Valuation Scheme introduced in 1843, which made all landlords responsible for the rates of holdings under £4. By 1845, 118 workhouses were established.

Obtaining relief in the earlier poorhouses and houses of industry was based on an assessment of an individual's level of destitution. A detailed debate over the method employed to assess destitution under the new poor law in Ireland arose. The poor law administrators sought to prevent dependency which would prove difficult in Ireland's case. Sir George Nicholls highlighted the differences between Ireland and England as regards the implementation of the Irish poor law. The immediate difference centred upon the extent of the deprivation amongst the pauper class. Thus, combined with the vast pauper population, it was not conducive to the establishment of a financially independent poor law. 'It thus appears that the workhouse system in England is used as a means, not so much of putting the able-bodied to work, as of putting them upon their own resources.'[17]

Accessing relief in an Irish union was modelled on the English concept of a destitute rule whereby 'the lot of the able-bodied inmate of the workhouse should be less tolerable than that of the lowest pauper outside.'[18] In essence the workhouses were perceived as a deterrent. A pauper's standard of living no matter how bad was often better than life in the workhouse. Only in such a catastrophe as arose in Ireland with the potato failures could paupers actually see any advantage in entering a workhouse. Nicholls found in Ireland the standard of paupers' 'mode of living' to be 'so unhappily low that the establishment of [a destitute rule] still lower is difficult.'[19] Nicholls aimed at relieving the plight of the genuinely proven destitute without encouraging the poor to become dependent upon the system.[20]

Two fundamental differences between the English and Irish poor law existed in relation to access to relief. Firstly, in Ireland all relief was to be administered wholly through the workhouses, whilst in England provision was made for outdoor relief. Secondly, in England every pauper had a legal right to receipt of relief. In Ireland this right was never introduced. The onus was placed on the individual to categorically prove his or her destitution. The public perceived the workhouse as the most abominable of places and it was always the final option. People sought poorly paid menial employment rather than avail of workhouse employment. Only the most destitute of the destitute applied for relief.

From the beginning workhouses created controversy. All agreed that the poor should receive aid or at least be encouraged to help themselves. Opponents of the system argued that if the poor received public assistance then some might avoid work or not work hard enough. In time it was felt the destitute Irish could become more burdensome 'on the backs of the Government and the ratepayers'. Another related concern was that the increasing numbers of Irish arriving in the English labour market would pose a 'threat to both wages and the established social order' thus necessitating state intervention.[21] It was therefore preferable to keep the paupers on the island rather than export the destitution to British unions.

Prudent economics and thriftiness were considered necessary to a successful implementation of the poor law. Admission to workhouses was curtailed where possible and inter-union migration was forbidden (this was to be transgressed during the famine years). The severity of the conditions in the workhouse acted as a deterrent to the populace. However with the onset of the famine 'under stringent and severe circumstances' such reticence evaporated and the workhouse, though detested, became the sole outlet of relief for Ireland's poor.[22]

This outlet for relief was purposely built and administered to exact and particular specifications. Workhouse construction prompted debate on the necessity for economic restraint while its external appearance was to appear imposing and serve as a deterrent to entry. The report of the poor law commissioners in 1839 states that the construction and design of the building was 'intended to be of the cheapest description compatible with durability; and its effect is aimed at by harmony of proportion and simplicity of arrangement, all decoration being studiously avoided.'[23]

George Wilkinson was assigned the task of designing the workhouses in Ireland. His reputation was familiar to the poor law commissioners, having worked on earlier projects concerning English workhouses. Wilkinson arrived in 1839 bringing his distinctive style to the Irish landscape. His buildings have 'lots of gables, and some decorative barge-boards on those gables in the main block in the front ... towers ... windows with mullions and transomes in them, large stone cross pieces actually in the window and with diamond glazing in them.'[24]

Wilkinson was burdened by poor law economic practices. The construction costs of the Irish workhouses were not to exceed two-thirds of those of similar workhouses in England and Wales. Cost efficiency was to be achieved through strict economy in both actual construction and in fitting out of the workhouse. Walls were usually left unplastered though whitewashed. The floors on the ground floor were of mortar or clay, as Wilkinson believed these surfaces not to be as cold as stone and less likely to decay than timber. Facilities inside the building were as meagre as the appearance was cold. Workhouses were deliberately designed in a manner that only those suffering acute deprivation and compelled by absolute necessity would seek admission to them. In July 1838 the relevant legislation was passed to allow admission to these un-inviting institutions. The act provided for the establishment of places of refuge, i.e. workhouses for the poor and the destitute, by the imposition of local taxes (rates).

By 1842 a total of 122 workhouses were complete. Despite the emphasis placed on cost efficiency the 'total cost in the end exceeded the first estimate of £1,000,000 by £145,000' and the speed with which they were built 'produced the inevitable crop of blunders and negligences.'[25]

By 1846 Cork union workhouse was one of twelve functioning workhouses in the county. It was the largest due to its large urban population. The union was declared on 3 April 1839 and consisted of fourteen electoral divisions each subdivided into electoral wards. The city electoral division was composed of twelve wards. Table 1 illustrates the electoral divisions of the Cork union and how they encompassed the city's hinterland and secondly the wards of the Cork city electoral division:

Table No. 1: Electoral divisions and electoral wards

Cork Union Electoral Divisions	Cork Electoral Division: Wards
1. Cork	1. Lee Ward
2. Iniscara	2. St Patrick's Ward
3. Carrigaline	3. Corn Market Ward
4. Cove	4. Glanmire Ward
5. Monkstown	5. St Finbar's Ward
6. Ballincollig	6. Mansion House Ward
7. White church	7. Curtain Ward
8. Glanmire	8. Exchange Ward
9. Blarney	9. Blackrock Ward
10. Grenagh	10. Bishopstown Ward
11. Carignavar	11. St Mary's Ward
12. Rathconney	12. St Anne's Ward
13. Kilgrane	
14. Inniskenny	*[Spelling as in original minute book]*

The purpose-built Cork workhouse based on Wilkinson's design was not completed until 1841. In the interim, the old house of industry (located off Douglas Street) functioned as a 'temporary workhouse'.[26] The first meeting of the guardians of Cork union workhouse was convened 'at the house of industry on 4 Tuesday June 1839 at noon'.[27] Mr Voules, a poor law commissioner, opened the proceedings and there followed lengthy discussions on the allocation of the various functions of the workhouse. A number of officers were elected, William Crawford was 'unanimously elected chairman with Samuel Lane and Joseph Hayes, vice chairman and deputy chairman respectively for the year ensuing'. It was agreed all three 'shall be members of all committees of this board unless expressly excepted'.[28] Furthermore it was deemed essential etiquette that at future meetings 'before the guardians proceed to business' that the chairman draw 'their attention to the rules of the house'.[29]

The necessary administrative functionaries of the workhouse were also decided – clerk, treasurer and a valuation committee. It was essential these officers be appointed expediently to give effect to the administration, organisation and financial direction of the workhouse. The main duties of the clerk involved recording the minutes and performing secretarial duties for the guardians. The treasurer and the valuation committee negotiated the rates and attained the security for the loan to continue construction of the new workhouse.

At the first meeting 'it was resolved that advertisements be inserted in the Cork papers announcing the intention of the board to proceed to the election of the clerk' at the next meeting.[30] On 17 June 1839 Karl Allen Deane was appointed to the office of clerk on a salary of £80 per annum. His primary function was to record the meetings and any union business in the minute books and the performance of various clerical duties. The method of his appointment, through advertisements in local papers, became the manner by which all subsequent employment, contracts and tenders to the workhouse were secured.

The office of treasurer was advertised simultaneously with the position of clerk. On 17 June it was announced 'that the National Bank of Ireland at Cork be the treasurer of the union'.[31] W. Hanley, assistant secretary to the poor law commissioners on 15 June sanctioned the bank's role as treasurer. However the commissioners raised the issue of the board entering into security with the bank. The guardians, thinking independently of the commissioners' advice, were resolute in their 'opinion that the National Bank being a joint stock company no security was required'.[32] With the treasurer assigned, the valuation committee began its calculations on the rates.

The seventeenth of June witnessed further developments in the financial formation of the union when the valuation committee presented its recommendations to the board. They recommended that 'the valuation of the house within the electoral division of Cork as well as the towns of Cove and Passage shall be two pence halfpenny for every house. Every building, be it dwelling house, warehouse or other tenement building having a separate entrance and every building or all buildings connected and to be connected with by one outward entrance be considered one house.'[33]

The valuation also recommended its entitlement to a sum of £2. 19s. per 1,000 statute acres to cover all expenses. Furthermore the committee advised that a board of superintendents was necessary to ensure 'sufficient accuracy'.

The board of guardians responded to the committee's counsel by agreeing to sit each afternoon at the house of industry, commencing 23 September. They sought to declare a rate 'with as little delay as possible' and permitted the books to be open for inspection so that 'the valuation for rating purposes may be seen' under 1 and 2 Victoria, Ch. 56, Sections 67 and 69.[34] A month later they modified their hours excepting Sundays and agreed 'that ratepayers may be at liberty to take extracts but in doing so will be restricted to the use of pencil'.[35]

The striking of the rate was not without complication or objections. The minutes state the urgency in declaring the rate and detail how certain wards, for example the Lee Ward, 'took up an entire day' to complete its inspection. Having ascertained for themselves 'that much discrepancy prevails in the value assigned to several lands and tenements' the guardians implemented the valuation committee's recommendation for a board of superintendents. It was resolved to request that the poor law commissioners sanction the appointment of a 'public officer to be charged with the inspection of the valuation' believing 'it was essential in order to secure a just valuation in all districts.'[36]

From the initial meetings of the Cork board of guardians two elements on the agenda of the board meetings are obvious. Firstly, there existed a willingness to follow poor law procedure in terms of establishing the union and secondly, they exhibited a tendency to modify certain aspects of the central poor law regime, to make it more applicable and relevant to their local concerns. The minutes frequently refer to the word 'just' – implying fairness. In the early meetings the board clashed with the poor law commissioners on the issue of fairness. The clauses of the poor relief act relating to the erection of workhouses 'provided an excellent basis for an almost indeterminable series of squabbles'.[37] One such issue concerned publicising the union's dealings.

Insofar as the general poor law principles on the establishment of the union were adhered to, the guardians felt the conduct and outcome of their meetings should remain under their control. In such a situation they had the freedom to invite whomever they chose to attend meetings. The question of local reporters attending meetings largely dominated the early proceedings and eventually the guardians recognised that the poor law commissioners in Dublin would always exercise ultimate control.

Those in attendance at the first meeting expressed their opinions on the necessity to publicise their activities and the new union. The fledgling administration in Cork faced its first contentious issue with the poor law commissioners. At the crux of the matter for the poor law commissioners was the necessity that the transactions of the Cork guardians remain private and confidential for fear of public misrepresentation. The very length of recorded proceedings devoted to this incident in the minute book testifies to the willingness of the Cork guardians to challenge the central poor law authority. They believed it to be in their own best interest to be a little transparent whilst inferring that the commissioners in Dublin did not understand the vagaries of each locale.

At the first meeting the issue of reporters was voiced by Mr Henry Murragh. Following protocol he asked the board to send a memorial to the poor law commissioners. In this he requested that 'the fourteenth clause of the second section of their orders applicable to their union be altered so as to admit the attendance of reporters for the newspapers under such restrictions and limitations as the commissioners may request'.[38] The commissioners' response was founded on their experience of the English model of poor relief whereby

> serious inconvenience was occasioned in England by permitting reporters and other persons unconnected with the business of the guardians to be present at the meetings, much of the transactions being of a private nature and as the examination of tenders, contractors, supplies, house accounts and other matters which publicity could not be properly given ... And experience of their prohibition have convinced them of their policy.[39]

Not content with the commissioners reply, the guardians appealed on 1 July only to have the commissioners reiterate their stance three weeks later again focusing on the English experience. Whilst conscious of the potential advantages they weighed these lightly,

> the continuous publicity which the Cork guardians at present desire would not promote the salutary object for which it is desired, while it may invite display in debate, it would be obstructive to the expeditious dispatch of business and … the experience they have had of its salutary operation in English workhouses confirms them in their resolution.[40]

Adamant in their conviction to allow reporters attend meetings the guardians again wrote to the poor law commissioners stating their order was not sustained. However the guardians accepted the commissioners' terms in 30 September, but a short time later having recognised 'that members were supplying partial reports to the press', they occasionally admitted reporters.[41] As other boards followed Cork's example the commissioners 'were compelled to beat a definite and dignified retreat'[42] and withdrew the order.[43]

This incident spans the first four months of the union's operation. It demonstrates that the attitudes of the commissioners were often at variance with those of the guardians. One commentator on the famine describes the commissioners' conceptions of their duties as akin to 'warriors in an administrative crusade' and not 'merely departmental officials engaged in guaranteeing the indigent Irishman from starvation.'[44] An element of determination and independent thought within the collective personality of the guardians became apparent, a determination, which was emphasised by the guardians' responses to later events.

In November 1839 the guardians voiced their annoyance with the commissioners over a particular incident whereby the commissioners exercised their administrational supremacy without notifying them. The matter centred on the erection of the new union workhouse. At issue were the legal rights of the commissioners and the lack of consultation with the Cork guardians. The guardians believed the construction of the house was within their remit. It was also the first reference in the minute books regarding the new workhouse.

The guardians felt undermined and 'surprised' as it came to their attention that an advertisement was placed in a Dublin journal on 16 November 1839 'for the erection of a workhouse proposed to be built in Cork'. The advertisement was perceived as an 'act of great discourtesy on the part of the commissioners', placed in the paper without any 'previous communication with the board and if not protested against would constitute a precedent detrimental to the interest of the ratepayers of the union.'[45] The vehemence of the proceedings illustrated that the guardians desired consultation at the very least, believing they were the best suited to discuss any such proposals for a new workhouse for their union. The guardians recognised the supremacy of the commissioners that in this instance gave them a 'legal right to determine the site and erect a workhouse'. The commissioners exercised a legal right to which the guardians could only concur. Dismayed with the lack of consultation, the guardians' argument referred to their 'own station and the protection of their constituents' believing that any 'expenditure so great as required for a workhouse shall not be entered upon without affording the board an opportunity of submitting their view and opinions as well as in regard to the site, as to the extent of accommodation necessary to be provided for the poor of the union.'[46]

Although somewhat disillusioned with the commissioners, the guardians put aside their grievances in favour of accelerating the process of construction. There was a prevailing mood of urgency amongst both the commissioners and guardians concerning the construction of the new workhouse. Hence by 12 February 1840 the guardians resolved unanimously to adopt the preliminary steps towards construction. The guidelines were issued in the act of 1838.

The initial financial arrangements concerning the union were described in a letter, received from the commissioners, urging a 'valuation of all rateable property in the union, by submitting all such valuations for inspection and revision and having also made a rate thereon and duly published notices of the making of such rates and proceeded to recommend proper persons to collect the same.'[47] This phase was essential. Once the collection procedure was arranged the rates could then be collected. The second financial issue concerned security for the advancement of a loan from the commissioners. Application was made to the Exchequer Bill Loan commissioners for 'a loan of sufficient sum to purchase the site, erect and fit out a new workhouse.'[48] Expedient clearance for the loan was urgent and subsequently a security for 'five thousand pounds part of such loan' was accepted.[49] As an adjunct the request stressed the house of industry be quickly declared the 'temporary workhouse' together with the 'issue of the necessary orders for relieving and setting the destitute poor to work therein pursuant to section 41 of the act.'[50]

The bureaucratic nature of the poor law system was perceived to be essential to its efficiency. It was evident at that early stage when the seal of the union was applied to all documentation. Official confirmation that the house of industry was a 'temporary workhouse', until the new house was built, arrived on 15 February together with the poor law regulations for the classification, admission and administration of the workhouse. These regulations would apply to the new house also. The regulations outlined six areas, which required the guardians' strict adherence.

Sections one to five applied to all workhouses under the poor law whilst section six specifically related to the Cork union. Each of the six sections was rigidly enforced, too often becoming a source of conflict amongst the guardians, torn between the reality they witnessed and the regulations which they were compelled to follow. The following transcript of a letter received from the poor law commissioners in Dublin regarding the establishment and administration of a union workhouse in the Cork union in the minutes gives an authentic insight into the workhouse regulations:[51]

19th Feb. 1840

Sir, The poor law commissioners having by order under seal bearing date 15th Feb., declared that the house of industry of Cork heretofore in part maintained by grants from the grand juries of the county and the city of

Cork, a temporary workhouse of the Cork union. We wish to direct the guardians attention to certain points requiring their especial consideration in administering the relief provided by the law.

1stly, the guardians are directed by the 41st section of the Irish Poor Act to take order for relieving in the workhouse the following descriptions of the destitute poor:

1) Those who by any reason of old age, infirmity or defect (bodily or mentally) may be unable to support themselves and also the destitute children.

2) Such other persons as the guardians shall deem to be destitute poor, unable from whatever cause to support themselves by their own industry or by other lawful means.

3) But, it is provided that if there shall not be sufficient accommodation in the workhouse for all the persons applying, whom the guardians all deem to be destitute, poor relief shall be given to such of the said persons as may be resident in the union in preference to those who may not be so resident.

2ndly, the above description of persons to be relieved in the order which they are here inserted and the preference which under the third head is to be given to those persons residing in the union, in cases where there is not in the workhouse room for all the destitute, whom may apply for relief must be observed by the guardians in strict conformity with the letter of the Act which expressly limits such preferences to cases where there is not sufficient accommodation for all who are deemed destitute.

3rdly, with respect to the destitute poor residing within the union to whom a preference is in such to be given, the commissioners consider that the guardians must exercise a fair and a reasonable discretion in enquiring into and deeming who are so resident and who are not and act accordingly.

4thly, great caution will be necessary at the onset in granting admission to the workhouse, even to those poor persons of whose destitution the guardians entertain no doubt, for a large influx at first, before due preparation has been made, and before the union functionaries have been properly trained and prepared might not only cause much suffering but also bring discredit to the workhouse system of relief.

5thly, the number of admissions should be regulated according to the means of accommodation actually existing in the workhouse, and all the inmates should be duly classified, clothed and provisioned in accordance with the workhouse regulations. For unless the organisation of the establishment be strictly enforced in every department as prescribed by the regulations, the workhouse will not be effective as a medium of relief, or as a test of destitution. Too much care cannot be given to this subject and more especially at the onset.

6thly, in the case of Cork this will be more especially necessary, the present workhouse being obviously defective in capacity and arrangement *as to deem it unfit from being permanently the workhouse of the union which requires a far larger workhouse and a more complete establishment for the due administration of relief and the commissioners have consented to declare that the present auxiliary house in compliance with the guardians earnestly request, in order to obviate inconveniences which it was apprehended would arise if the declaration was delayed until the new workhouse now in progress of building shall be completed. Under such circumstances the greatest care will be required to enforce order and to guard against the laxity of discipline and other evils too likely associated with 1,000 or 1,500 inmates lodged and fed in a building in all respects so very imperfect and insufficient. The commissioners also wish to call to the particular attention of the guardians to that portion of the order containing the workhouse rules which prescribes the mode of keeping and auditing the union accounts and without the careful observance of which from the commencement much confusion and inconvenience will arise. The several forms have been prepared with great care and will be simple and effective in objects to be contemplated, similar attention will be requisite in enforcing the workhouse regulations and it should be distinctly understood by the officers of the union and others that any breach of the commissioners' instructions will subject the offender to the penalties which will be strictly enforced under the provisions of the Act.*

By the order of the board
Mr Hanley,
Assistant Secretary.

Source: BG 69 A 1, week ending 24 Feb. 1840

Section six of the commissioners' letter details the areas most likely to pose problems for the Cork union. It was perceived that accommodation would pose the greatest problem. Upon receipt of inmates the present house of industry would be 'obviously defective in capacity and arrangement as' to deem it unfit as the permanent workhouse of the union. The commissioners considered any delay of the declaration of the union (until the new workhouse off Evergreen Street was completed) as unfeasible.[52] Therefore the commissioners emphasised the importance of strict adherence to the rules and the need to 'guard against the laxity of discipline and other evils too likely associated with 1,000 or 1,500 inmates lodged and fed in a building in all respects so very imperfect and insufficient.'[53]

In regulating the economy of this 'imperfect' building the guardians' attention was drawn to the section of the order detailing fiscal procedures. Procedures required 'careful observance' and the necessary forms for bookkeeping and auditing of accounts were prepared to be 'simple and effective in the objects to be contemplated'. Urging the importance of fiscal scrutiny, the commissioners stated that 'any breach will subject the offender to the penalties which will be strictly enforced under the provisions of the Act'.[54]

The first inmates of the union workhouse located at the house of industry were admitted on 1 March 1840. Within seven months the necessary functionaries of master, ward matron, ward staff and medical staff were all appointed. Contractors tendered for supplies of milk and other provisions. In the course of the following year, extensions were added to facilitate pauper admissions highlighting the need for expedient completion of the new workhouse.

The new purpose-built workhouse opened in December 1841. Designed by Wilkinson, its shape and detail were reminiscent of the English workhouse. The location of the new workhouse emphasised the geographical expansion of the city. A map of 1827 shows the city's southward expansion ending near the house of industry. By 1841 the city had extended further south. The new workhouse was located at the confluence of all the main routes to the county. The site – a bogland off Evergreen Street – was chosen and it was in close proximity to the house of industry. It was in the vicinity of Ballyphehane and Ballinlough.[55]

The new house boasted an increased capacity, designed to hold 2,000 inmates, an increase of 500. In its early years it became apparent that its capacity was inadequate. William Thackeray visited Cork in 1842 and commented on this, 'the poorhouse newly established cannot hold a fifth part of the poverty of this great town.'[56] He further noted the paupers' attitudes to the workhouse; 'the people like their freedom, such as it is and prefer to starve and be ragged, they will not go to the workhouse except at the greatest extremity and leave then on the slightest chance of subsistence elsewhere.'[57] Thackeray echoed Sir George Nicholls' opinion described in a letter by W. Stanley (assistant secretary to the commissioners) to Cork. He outlined that 'Mr Nicholls states in his first report that the Irishman has a natural reluctance to become a poorhouse inmate and nothing but absolute destitution, starvation will force him to encounter the discipline, the irksome regulations, the disagreeable labour and the confinement of such a house under the present system.'[58] Table 2 compares the final entry in the minutes of inmate figures of the temporary house (week ending 29 November) with the first entry of the new house (week ending 6 December). Two key points are evident, firstly, the temporary house of industry was insufficient and secondly, the new house was almost full within one week.

The number of inmates resident in the temporary workhouse on the week ending 29 November 1841 already exceeded the capacity of 1,500 (including sheds and auxiliary buildings). In 1841 the demand for pauper accommodation outstripped availability. A constant demand for workhouse accommodation, despite the paupers' reluctance to enter such an institution, alludes to the numbers of paupers in Cork city in 1841. One can only imagine how this need for accommodation would reach crisis point with the excessive and severe overcrowding attributable to the famine.

Table No. 2: Comparison of figures between temporary workhouse (29 November 1841) and the newly built workhouse (6 December 1841)

Week ending	Number Previous Week	Admitted	Died	Discharged	Total
29 Nov.	1,829	163	9	112	1,871
6 Dec.(1841)	1,871	174	7	86	1,952

Source: Compiled from figures in minute book BG69 A2

Three-quarters of Cork's population formed the pauper class in the pre-famine years. Cork was 'swarming with life, but of a frightful kind that no pen need care to describe; alleys … odours … rags. In some [quarters] they say not the policeman but the priest can only penetrate'.[59] Thackeray, on his tour through the county noted that the Cork paupers eked out an existence elsewhere amid charitable and not so charitable institutions. Cork county gaol was praised for its quality diet in 1842 and was 'so neat, spacious and comfortable that we can only pray to see every cottager in the county as cleanly well lodged and well fed as the convicts are.'[60]

With a such a large proportion of paupers, it is easy to understand why the new workhouse was insufficient in 1841. Even with its increased capacity for 2,000 inmates it was still deficient. The guardians could not aspire to make a difference in terms of reducing the numbers of destitute within the city. Their principal aim was to ease their immediate distress.

Such desires were frustrated. Inmates in the new workhouse during the first week numbered 1,871. The figure would have been higher was it not for the inmates who absconded while being transferred from the house of industry to the new workhouse. Poor law bureaucrats saw the incident as an obvious lack of discipline and organisation. The master, Mr Buckley, reported to the commissioners on the 'able-bodied paupers [who] absconded on their way from the old to the new house'. He further infers that it was difficult to adequately transfer about 1,900 paupers – 'all in one day!'[61] Since unnecessary expenditure was frowned upon by the poor law authorities the master's report outlines his particular worry that the inmates escaped wearing the workhouse uniform. Nevertheless the uniform would readily identify the escapees and Sub-Inspector Wright in Waterford duly arrested three of them, namely Peter Ellis, George Bedmont and Denis Maude. Once returned to Cork workhouse they were prosecuted for theft of union clothing. The penal nature of the institution was clearly emphasised from the outset.

Regimentation and discipline were fundamental principles of the poor law and Mr Voules, assistant commissioner at Clancool, Bandon, wrote to the guardians desiring 'the names of the officers of the establishment through whose omission or neglect' the inmates escaped.[62] He also sent a letter outlining his recommendations and immediate alterations to the new house to increase its efficiency in fulfilling the aims of the poor law:

Letter received from Assistant Commissioner Voules, Esq.

Clancool, Bandon,

January 12th 1842

Gentlemen,

I beg to submit the following suggestions arising out of a recent inspection of your union and to invite your co-operation in giving them immediate effect.

Firstly – the boundary wall or fence to enclose the whole of the land purchased for the union should be completed without delay. This is essential to the security of the house and the property therein, to the preservation of order and discipline, and to the employment of the able-bodied inmates who will thus be provided with labour within the walls. These objects I think would be further promoted by the erection of a suitable residence (opening inwards) for one of the ward or work masters of the establishment.

I decree the boundary wall of such importance that I would strongly urge the guardians to make application for a further advance for its erection, before it is too late, as if the building is postponed and I am sure the necessity for it will be every day more apparent, the charge of its construction must fall upon the rates.

Secondly – that the master of the workhouse should be authorised to select such a number of persons out of the house (that is not being inmates) as will enable him to ensure and guarantee the preservation of order and the performance of labour and for whom he will be responsible.

Thirdly – that all the male inmates of the house not absolutely incapacitated by age or disease and including boys should be required to work for such time and with such intervals as the guardians (with the advice of the medical officers) shall determine, in levelling the inequalities of the site and converting it into a state of cultivation and into cleansing and washing yards. No person need be required to exert himself beyond his strength but each person must be required to do something and this is not only with a view to the dissipation of previously formed habits of idleness and inactivity but to the preservation of the general health.

Fourthly – that all the bedridden male inmates should occupy one room if possible on the ground floor instead of being as now scattered over the whole of the dormitories thereby preventing their being duly ventilated and cleaned. The same observation applies to bedridden females.

Fifthly – the cleansing and the scouring of the male wards with the passages, stairs etc. Connecting therein should be performed entirely by males instead of females as is now practised. The reasons for this are obvious and the precedent of seamen on board ships and inmates of other large establishments shows its practicability.

Sixthly – the use of tobacco should be strictly prohibited except as a medicine, in which case its administration should be confined to a stated time and a detached place instead of its being used in the wards.

Seventhly – copies of the orders in reference to the punishment for insubordination and the 58th and 59th Section of the Act should be placarded in each ward. The punishment prescribed by the orders should be promptly applied as proof of the offence being committed and to its repetition or in flagrant cases Sections 58th and 59th should be resorted to.

W. J. Voules

Source: minute book of Cork union workhouse, BG69 A2,
week ending 17 January 1842

Voules considered his recommendations important and they 'should in all cases be promptly applied.[63] 'One suggestion referred to the need for spatial efficiency. He advocated that all incapacitated and bedridden men and women should occupy single dormitories as opposed to being scattered throughout the house. Spatial considerations were important since inmate numbers exceeded capacity constantly from 10 January until 25 April when a seasonal reduction occurred. The highest instance during this period was the week ending 21 March 1842 when 2,266 inmates were resident in the house.

Fiscal restraint, crime and punishment, rules, discipline and spatial consideration were constantly debated by the board of guardians. The new workhouse had many obvious defects and inefficiencies. It had an increased inmate capacity of only 500 to bring the total capacity to 2,000, an underestimation even in 1841. These inefficiencies perceived as teething problems in 1841 became chronic during 1845–50. They stretched the resources of the administration resulting in Cork union workhouse becoming what one dignitary later described as a 'chamber of horrors'.[64]

2

THE ROLE OF CORK UNION WORKHOUSE DURING THE FAMINE

'Historical "Ifs" are fascinating. If the workhouses had not been introduced would Ireland have ultimately benefited? Or did the presence of these buildings during the Famine save thousands of lives?'[1]

The workhouses of Ireland were always perceived as the last resort in cases of destitution. The Irish pauper class were disinclined to enter workhouses. This reluctance was attributed to the Destitute Rule, which stated that workhouse conditions were of a standard greatly inferior to those of the lowest class of pauper outside. Entrance to the workhouse in the pre-famine years affirmed both a person's destitution and his failure to provide for himself and his family. For the famine victims the workhouse provided the aura of hope and an attempt at survival. With the advent of the famine, entering the workhouse was not an affirmation of their destitution, which was by then indubitable, rather they were spurred on by an instinct to survive.

This urge to survive can be clearly seen by examining the evidence and the figures calculated from the official proceedings together with individual case studies of some inmates. In reality the workhouse did not guarantee survival, whether in time of famine or not. Conditions within the workhouse were conducive to the generation and spread of disease. Such pestilent conditions often accelerated the timeframe in which diseases proved fatal. Therefore the role of the workhouse in the famine years was accentuated greatly. Paradoxically as an institution it aimed to improve the lot of the pauper but by its very nature accelerated the incidence of death. This chapter looks at both of these paradoxical roles by evaluating the evidence such as the admission, discharge and mortality figures. It should be noted that this is probably the first time that the numerical evidence contained within the Cork union minute books has been collated for the famine period in a painstaking attempt at clarifying what exactly happened within the house. It highlights the magnitude of the plight of the famine victims.

In September 1845 the potato blight had 'unequivocally declared itself in Ireland, where will Ireland be in the event of a universal potato rot?'[2] This foreboding question cited in the *Gardener's Chronicle*, was applicable to the majority of Ireland's population who were utterly reliant on the potato for their physical and financial existence. 'How an island which is said to be an integral part of the richest empire on the globe – and the most fertile part of that empire ... should in five years lose two and a half millions of its people (more than one-fourth) by hunger, and fever the consequence of hunger, and flight beyond the sea to escape hunger'.[3] This was the question that John Mitchel, Young Irelander, and outspoken advocate of tenant-farmers, the sentiment of which is still evident today when one thinks of the enormity of the famine.[4] One response was the flight to the workhouse wherein the famished paupers hoped to gain respite from the menace of famine while at all times the workhouse remained in their consciousness as the last resort. Mitchel described the enormity of the flight into workhouses as being 'like a Temple erected to the fates, or like the fortress of Giant Despair, whereinto he draws them one by one, and devours them there.'[5] Cork union workhouse built to accommodate 2,000 paupers became the main source of relief for thousands. By 1846 workhouse relief, previously to be avoided, seemed to become attractive.

Admission figures for the period 1845–50 indicate a change in the pauper mindset regarding their perception of relief. An analysis of such figures confirms the double-sided role of Cork workhouse in both alleviating short-term destitution whilst often contributing to an inmate's ill-health and death. Additionally, the evidence alludes to the sociological impact of the famine in areas of gender and pauper classification whilst also highlighting the famine's fast moving progress.

The number of admissions in 1845 reflected those of the previous year. The blight 'unequivocally declared' in September 1845 did not impact upon the pauper class until 1846. The admissions for January to April 1845 were higher than admissions from September to December 1845. There were three reasons for this. Firstly, there was a history of previous crop shortages usually of a short duration and though seemingly famine-like conditions often prevailed they were not as catastrophic as the blight which arrived in 1845. The revisitation of the same blight again in 1846 sounded the commencement proper of the famine. The failure in 1845 was initially perceived as just another crop failure. Recovery would follow but many felt it was just another visitation from God. Secondly, paupers consumed their limited reserves in the early months of the famine viewing it as a time of scarcity as opposed to the initial stages of a countrywide famine. Thirdly, the human body's ability to adapt to a reduced intake of food for some time without incurring adverse effects to health. Cutting the intake of food by half over a period of time (approx. six months) reduces body weight by one-fourth. The stability in the admission numbers of 1845 may be viewed somewhat as a norm for pre-famine times. Richard Dowden, Lord Mayor of Cork, wrote to the government in London outlining his fears on the initial scarcity of the potato. He referred to the potato as the 'Great Staple of Irish existence'. If this was the lord mayor's view of the crisis in 1845, the reader can only but imagine the horrors to unfold in the following years:

> May it please your Excellency: the very great and it is to be feared well-founded alarm which the decay in the potato crop has produced among the people induces me to add to the number of communications which must have been made to your Excellency, praying your Excellency's attention to … the probable prospects of the great staple of Irish existence … to endure the severe visitation of scarcity of their only food. I am sure the government has already been prompt and ready to consider well a subject in which the health and peace of the nation is necessarily involved.[6]

Fig. 1: Monthly admissions to Cork workhouse 1845

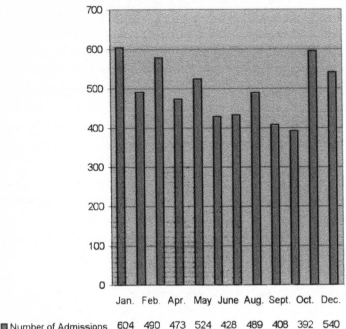

	Jan.	Feb.	Apr.	May	June	Aug.	Sept.	Oct.	Dec.
■ Number of Admissions	604	490	473	524	428	489	408	392	540

The gender make-up of the workhouse is evident from Figure 2. The line graph shows a consistently higher rate of female to male admissions. The underlying reasons for this higher rate of female admissions are many. From studying the workhouse registers the description of women upon admittance gives an insight into this statistic. Each inmate seeking entry to the house was asked on arrival a number of questions. The answers were noted in the relevant category of the register. The officers requested the following information: age; sex; religion; marital status; if children, their names and ages and/or whether orphaned; if abandoned or deserted, where the father of the children could possibly be; occupation; any health problems and address. The officers also had a category for 'general appearance' at admission. The clerical officer noted the appearance in terms such as 'haggard', 'old', 'able-bodied', 'lame' and 'rashy' were among some of the diverse descriptions which one can see on looking through these books.

Many women and children were deserted while others sought to gain access to relief under false pretences of desertion, while their husbands worked abroad. Even those falsifying desertion highlighted the extent of the hardships endured by the lower echelons of Irish society. Given the limitations of workhouse relief, financial gain was scarcely a motive. Cramped communal conditions, the separation of families and absence of adequate sanitation facilities were equally uninviting. The Public Works schemes were directed towards manual male labour. If these were the trends in 1845, how much worse would they be in 1846?

In 1846 these gender trends continued but at a more accelerated pace. From January 1846 admissions of persons above the age of fifteen steadily increased. In August of that year the pace of

Fig. 2: Numbers of males and females admitted during 1845

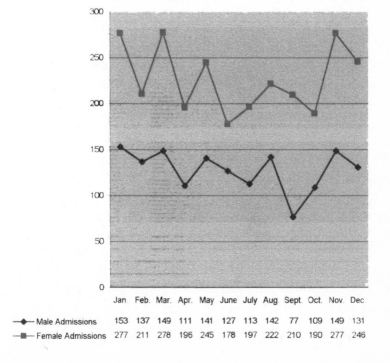

	Jan.	Feb.	Mar.	Apr.	May	June	July	Aug.	Sept.	Oct.	Nov.	Dec.
Male Admissions	153	137	149	111	141	127	113	142	77	109	149	131
Female Admissions	277	211	278	196	245	178	197	222	210	190	277	246

admissions radically escalated to an unprecedented point peaking in October and November with figures of 2,358 and 2,146 respectively (see table 3). These figures have been compiled from the figures of admissions for each week during 1846.

Table No. 3: Admission numbers 1846

Month	Admissions
Jan.	779
Feb.	893
March	924
April	1,048
May	1,141
June	826
July	832
Aug.	1,231
Sept.	1,137
Oct.	2,358
Nov.	2,146
Dec.	2,040
Total	**15,355**

These increases were largely the consequences of the second crop failure combined with the paupers' depleted reserves in meeting the crisis. Much of the grain and reserves of other produce was consumed during the previous shortage. William Bishop was an inspecting official for the relief commission, he reported on the shortages of crops and the looming shortage of bread, with over ten tonnes being consumed in Cork city on a daily basis in December 1846:

> The same class of grain crops produced last year are now in progress, but not to a greater extent. More turnips are being sown than last year – grain is fast disappearing ... Home produce will now be consumed ... Bread stuffs consumed in Cork and vicinity daily 100 tons – the merchants have not more than 4,000 tons in store. Delivery of wheat is small, farms having used much of it themselves.[7]

The poor law commissioner, Joseph Burke described the distress which he witnessed in Cork in November 1846 and his fears for the next year which was to be the worst year referred to as Black '47. On his travels through Ireland he noted Cork to be 'an extensive district, the present condition of the people and judging of their future prospects, afforded me information on the subject which may not be open to or taken advantage of by others – although bad as is the state of the people I dread that it will be worse next year'.[8] The second potato failure ensured that the wave of admissions would increase to an uncontrollable level. Rising numbers exerted pressure on the guardians in the discharge of their duties so much so that pressure forced Captain William Martin, guardian of the Glanmire electoral district, to tender his resignation. He voiced the opinion that some of the guardians are 'little acquainted with the mental pressures to which the officers of the house are now subjected and they are more detrimental to their health than any bodily exertion.'[9] He was asked by the board a week later to reconsider and to clarify his reasons. In his returning letter he outlined the inadequacies of the house as regards the increasing number of women. He stated that so great was the number of women entering the workhouse that there was not enough work for which to engage them. Despite the 'season of scarcity', Martin was a traditional upholder of all that the poor law stood for, consequently he viewed the lack of work for all female inmates as an 'idleness' which the poor law strove to avoid. He believed the women should be employed more effectively and could alleviate the pressures on the officers. He felt that having 'such a number of able-bodied women in the house without employment is contrary to what providence ordained and it is the bounded duty of the guardians to remedy this.'[10]

His opinions were not unfounded. An analysis of the total number of women remaining in the workhouse each Saturday substantiates Martin's opinion. In August 1846 women (above fifteen years) composed 74 per cent of inmates in Cork union workhouse as is clear from table 4:

Table No. 4: Percentage composition of men and women (above the age of fifteen) in Cork union workhouse for 1846

Date	1846 (Men) %	1846 (Women) %
January	26	74
February	27	73
March	26	74
April	28	72
May	26	74
June	25	75
July	27	73
August	26	74
September	26	74
October	26	74
November	26	74
December	26	74

From November 1845 to December 1846, 65 per cent of all admissions to Cork workhouse were women. The ratio of women to men seeking admission varied between 2.6 in April and 2.9 in November 1846 (as evident from tables 5 and 6).

Table No. 5: Ratio of aged and infirm men to women in Cork workhouse based on the weekly average each month. Calculated from the minute books BG69 A4 to BG69 A12. Note: in 1846 the minute books do not differentiate between the able-bodied and the aged/infirm. All male and female inmates are classified according to age; all males and females above fifteen years of age. The 1846 figures are based on total weekly averages of all men and women above 15 years.

Date	1846	1847	1849	1850	1851
January	1: 2.8	1: 2.8		1: 1.8	1: 1.1
February	1: 2.7	1: 3		1: 1.8	1: 1.8
March	1: 2.8	1: 3	1: 1.6	1: 2	1: 1.8
April	1: 2.6	1: 3.8	1: 1.5	1: 1.6	1: 1.7
May	1: 2.7	1: 3	1: 1.4	1: 1.8	1: 1.9
June	1: 2.9	1: 2.9	1: 1.5	1: 2.4	1: 1.9
July	1: 2.7		1: 1.6	1: 2.5	1: 2.2
August	1: 2.8		1: 2	1: 6.2	1: 2.5
September	1: 2.9		1: 2.6	1: 5.8	1: 2.5
October	1: 2.9		1: 1.8	1: 5.4	1: 2.6
November	1: 2.9		1: 1.7	1: 2.5	1: 2.5
December	1: 2.8		1: 1.6	1: 2.8	1: 2.9

Table No. 6: Ratio of able-bodied men to women in Cork workhouse based on weekly averages each month. Calculated from the minute books BG69 A4 to BG69 A12. Note: in 1846 the minute books do not differentiate between the able-bodied and the aged/infirm. All male and female inmates are classified according to age; all males and females above fifteen years of age. The 1846 figures are based on total weekly averages of all men and women above fifteen years.

Date	1846	1847	1849	1850	1851
January	1: 2.8	1: 2.8		1 : 2	1: 1.1
February	1: 2.7	1: 3		1: 2.1	1: 1.8
March	1: 2.8	1: 3	1: 2.5	1: 2.2	1: 1.8
April	1: 2.6	1: 3.8	1: 2.4	1: 2.1	1: 1.7
May	1: 2.7	1: 3	1: 2.1	1: 2.1	1: 1.9
June	1: 2.9	1: 2.9	1: 1.8	1: 2.1	1: 1.9
July	1: 2.7		1: 1.8	1: 2.1	1: 2.2
August	1: 2.8		1: 1.8	1: 2.1	1: 2.5
September	1: 2.9		1: 1.6	1: 2.1	1: 2.5
October	1: 2.9		1: 1.8	1: 2.2	1: 2.6
November	1: 2.9		1: 1.9	1: 2.2	1: 2.5
December	1: 2.8		1: 1.8	1: 2.1	1: 2.9

Both the female and the male admission figures mirror one another in their gradients when plotted against one another. This suggests that admissions for each gender were affected similarly.

Fig. 3: Proportion of female to male admissions November 1845 – December 1846

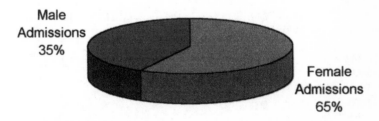

Male Admissions 35%

Female Admissions 65%

The only decline in admissions was a slight lull experienced in June and July of 1846 prior to the second crop failure. In 1846 admissions to the house numbered 15,355.[11] However the 'excessive crowding' witnessed at the beginning of 1846 proved to be a hint of what was to follow in the autumn of that year with the second crop failure.[12] There was to be increased mortality when coupled with the inferior and substandard sanitation facilities and the provision of inadequate medical relief.[13] 1846 saw a corresponding rise in the incidence of fever epidemics and associated diseases. The Fever Act of 1846 extended fever accommodation in terms of wooden sheds, which were usually constructed adjacent to the fever hospitals. Unfortunately, no such sheds were built adjacent to the workhouse. It was some time before 'fever' victims of the workhouse were sent to isolated sheds nearby. Neither did the actual number of medical officers available to deal with the crises increase sufficiently to contain such epidemics.

The geographical location of the workhouse was in itself a prejudicial influence on inmate health. Dampness was rampant in the area where 'the poorhouse in Cork is situated on the verge of the unwholesome, death-producing bog of Ballyphehane'.[14] The reluctance of the commissioners to sanction additional buildings other than the fever hospital until 1847 emphasised a bureaucratic and ideological inertia. The house capacity was 2,000 (see table 7). The commissioners responded in February 1846 to the guardians on the issue of increasing admissions. They cautioned against the 'evil' of overcrowding. They were aware that pestilence and death would accompany excessive overcrowding.

Table No. 7: Numbers of inmates for a selected day, Nov. 1845–Aug. 1846

	8 Nov. 1845	20 Dec.	14 Feb.	21 Mar.	25 Apr.	30 May	27 June	1 Aug. 1846
Number of inmates in workhouse	1,856	2,050	2,428	2,633	2,707	2,635	2,595	2,619
Inmate capacity of workhouse	2,000	2,000	2,000	2,000	2,000	2,000	2,000	2,000

By 1847 it was obvious that the Cork workhouse fulfilled two roles. It was by design an agent of relief and through lack of spatial awareness and planning, at a time of distress it became a catalyst for disease and ultimately death. The devastation of Black '47 was total. Unfortunately, the evidence for this period is based on the six-month period of January to June as minute books for the remainder of 1847 are missing. In six months 7,817 persons sought admission to the workhouse. A record number of 2,714 admissions occurred in January as outlined in the graph shown in figure 4.

Fig. 4: Admissions for the period January to June 1847

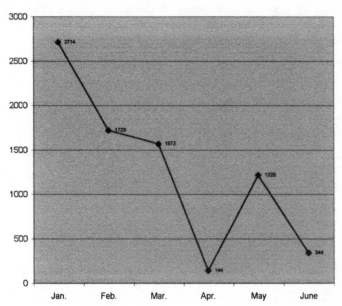

The average number of inmates resident for that month was 4,345. Joseph Burke, assistant commissioner, noted the excessive distress of January 1847 and the impact this was having on the workhouse.[15] Following a meeting with the board of guardians he penned the following on the 18 January:

> Gentlemen, I this day attended the meeting of the guardians of the Cork union. The number of the inmates in the workhouse and in the two additional wards has now reached 5,310 – 868 of whom were admitted within the last fortnight – the medical officers, having given in their report, a copy of which I forward, the propriety of allowing further admissions was discussed, where it was agreed not to exceed the present number in the house and that admissions could only be allowed as discharges occurred … a

resolution was also adopted by the guardians that the present state of the poor law was quite inadequate to meet the unprecedented destitution which now prevails. It must certainly be admitted that the poor law was introduced to meet the destitution of an ordinary year – but not to provide against a famine. If the guardians of the Cork union could procure further accommodation I am certain that the numbers that would avail themselves of workhouse relief would be double or treble what it is now and then would come the question of how funds were to be procured, as adequate means to meet such an extensive system of relief could not be obtained by making heavy rates on an impoverished people …

A figure of 4,345 resident inmates was hugely disproportionate to the capacity of the house, which was increased from a capacity of 2,000 to 2,800 inmates (see table 8). An increase of 800 in the house capacity could not hope to improve such cramped conditions. 1847 recorded an unprecedented number of deaths within this six-month period as will be discussed later. The number of inmates in the house in February 1847 totalled 5,310, an increase of 1,000 on the previous month. The figure remained at the same level for March; almost double the capacity of the house was within the confines of the institution.

Table No. 8: Weekly average of inmates per month in the workhouse

1847	Jan.	Feb.	Mar.	Apr.	May	June
Inmates per month	4,345	5,310	5,207	4,343	3,830	3,254
Inmate capacity	2,800	2,800	2,800	2,800	2,800	2,800

There are three reasons for the increase in the number of inmates.

Firstly, the numbers of admissions for February and March 1847 were still high being 1,723 and 1,672 respectively. Inmate numbers continued to rise as inmates prolonged their terms of residence in the workhouse. Typically an inmate remained in the house for between one week to a month. With the increased severity of 1847 people preferred to remain in the house rather than face life outside. Secondly, the majority of adult admissions were of the category known as 'aged and infirm' and consisted largely of women. During 1847 the ratio of aged and infirm women to men was sporadic between 2.8 to 3.8 (see tables 5 & 6). Thirdly, other relief charities and soup kitchens were alleviating the conditions of the starving outside thereby helping to reduce the numbers of paupers seeking admission to the workhouse. The soup kitchen in Adelaide Street was one of the busiest in Cork. Were it not for its existence and other relief organisations in the city then the number of workhouse inmates would surely have been much greater.

The trend of a higher admission figure in the overall female groupings was observed in 1847 again. In January 1,048 of 2,714 admissions were women aged above fifteen. As stated, a large proportion were aged and infirm women, the remainder were women with families whose husbands had deserted, or died.

The fluctuations in the severity of the famine were reflected by male and female admissions. In table 9 a sharp decline occurred in April as calculated from the returns in the minute books.

Table No. 9: Male & female admission figures (above fifteen years of age) for January to June 1847

1847	Jan.	Feb.	Mar.	Apr.	May	June
Male admissions	633	378	420	47	362	107
Female admissions	1,048	658	575	51	414	138

The minutes record only ninety-eight adult admissions for April. This glaring reduction occurred because the workhouse closed its doors temporarily and engaged in outdoor relief. Additionally, the frequency of discharges increased. Admission figures advanced to 1,220 in May but were followed by the usual seasonal decline. The decline amounted to almost one-third. Many inmates sought shelter and convalescence within the house during the harsher months. Improved climatic conditions were an incentive for many to leave the workhouse even if their own situation outside the house was little better. For the vast majority of paupers workhouse conditions were marginally better than those they left. However the margin of improvement was sometimes negated by the fact that the workhouse revealed its sinister ability to spread rampant disease and more often than not indirectly contributed to many deaths.

Natural disasters are usually accompanied by an epidemic. Cholera appeared in the late spring of 1849. The calculations for 1849 are based on available records for March to December as the minutes are missing. In comparison to the admissions of 1847, the figure for 1849 appeared to have undergone convulsions. The reasoning for this was an increase in the house capacity. At this stage discernable efforts were made to increase accommodation. From 1847 to 1849 capacity varied from 2,800 to 6,300. Construction of auxiliary buildings occurred in 1848. These efforts relieved the pressure both on inmates and staff, whilst simultaneously providing additional places for destitute paupers.

Table No. 10: Admissions to Cork workhouse – March to end November 1849

Mar.	Apr.	May	June	July	Aug.	Sept.	Oct.	Nov.
1,575	2,472	2,901	3,331	1,386	1,332	1,585	1,431	1,739

Table 10 illustrates a sharp rise in admissions for March to June 1849. An external factor had therefore provoked hundreds to seek admission to the workhouse. In the city cholera was raging. The workhouse, with its adjoining infirmary and fever hospital, appeared to be a sanctuary for cholera victims yet the actual conditions in the house were conducive to the spread of cholera and invariably those seeking admission contracted the disease they strove to avoid. The effect of the 1848 building programme allowed for increased admissions, though with no discernible improvement in sanitation and hygiene. As a result once the cholera established a foothold in the workhouse in 1849 it had a larger host on which to prey and spread.

Numbers peaked with 3,331 admissions in June coinciding with the cholera epidemic. 'The premonitory signs' were visible in April according to the workhouse physicians.[16] By July the crisis abated, denoted by a consequential drop in admissions. This decrease also reflected the seasonal adjustments. From August to

November the figures in table 10 exhibit a modicum of stability in the admission figures. Such stability hinted that the worst excesses of the famine were over. Table 11 is further witness to the normalisation of workhouse conditions after the cholera epidemic. The number of inmates had stabilised to a point coinciding with the level of accommodation available. House capacity was reduced in August as the epidemic had dissipated. Some of the temporary sheds and auxiliary buildings no longer needed were removed. The guardians reacted quicker to this improvement in the general health of the house in contrast to their tardiness in dealing efficiently with the deterioration in conditions during the early years.

Table No. 11: Inmate numbers, March–Dec. 1849, and house capacity figures

1849	Mar	Apr.	June	July	Aug.	Sept.	Oct.	Dec.
No. of inmates in workhouse	6,305	6,617	6,911	6,805	4,506	3,972	4,218	4,770
Inmate capacity of workhouse	6,300	6,300	6,300	7,100	7,100	3,050	4,100	4,700

The extent to which the famine impacted on the house in 1849 appeared to be not as severe as in 1847. Although 'convulsions' occurred in the numbers seeking admission a semblance of stability was apparent.[17] Overcrowding in the workhouse was less pronounced in terms of the ratio of admissions to capacity by 1849. This is obvious by comparing the periods March to June in 1847 and 1849.

In the period March to June 1847 there were 16,634 admissions of persons over fifteen years of age. The house capacity at that time was 2,800. Thus the ratio of admissions to capacity was 1:5.95. For the same period in 1849, admissions amounted to 18,891 while the increased capacity was 6,300 and the ratio of admissions to capacity was 1: 1.6. In spatial terms, 1849 sought to accommodate the inmates more humanely than in 1847. Table 11 clearly illustrates this point. From July to December the inmates in the workhouse were facilitated in accordance with house capacity.

The stability that occurred in the second half of 1849 con-

tinued into 1850. There was an increase in January, a usual occurrence irrespective of the existence of famine conditions. Thereafter it declined and followed the usual seasonal lull from May to
July and the predictable autumnal increase but the numbers continued to remain stable. Admission trends for 1850 suggest that by
then the actual famine was no longer influencing the systematic
admissions to the house. It was the legacy and the impact of the
famine that affected the admissions. In 1850 and 1851 the pattern
of higher female to male admissions continued but at a more pronounced level (see figures 5 and 6).

The gender composition of the house became more pronounced within the class of able-bodied women. Table 12 shows a
much higher composition of women in the Cork workhouse in the
first half of 1851. This is partially attributable to desertion, death
and the emigration of many spouses during the famine years. The
increased proportion of deserted mothers is further discussed in
the following chapters.

Fig. 5: Male and female admissions for 1850

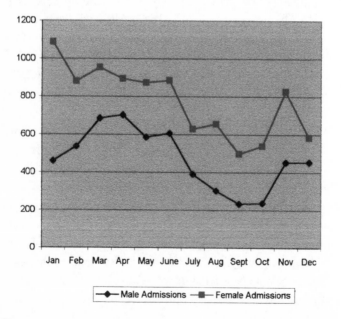

Fig.6: Male and female admissions for 1851

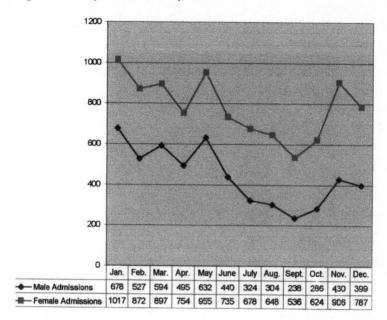

	Jan.	Feb.	Mar.	Apr.	May	June	July	Aug.	Sept.	Oct.	Nov.	Dec.
Male Admissions	678	527	594	495	632	440	324	304	238	286	430	399
Female Admissions	1017	872	897	754	955	735	678	648	536	624	906	787

By 1851 the impact of the famine had forcibly altered the role of the house. It had by then become more ameliorative to the inmates' distress than in the previous years when it had been hampered by much bureaucratic bungling. Its role was also impeded by the institutional conditions, which exerted negative influences upon the health of inmates (outlined in chapter three).

The incidence of death can be analysed through available records. Death and the accelerated pace of death were synonymous with life within the workhouse. Its acceleration was so great that at times the issue of burials and burial grounds proved problematical for the guardians. Canon John O'Rourke reminisced:

> Some idea of the dreadful mortality then prevalent in Cork may be found in the fact that in one day thirty-six bodies were interred in the same grave and from the autumn 1846 to May 1847, 10,000 persons were interred in Father Mathew's cemetery in Cork that he was forced to close it.[18]

Table No. 12: Male and female composition of the workhouse in 1851

Date	1851 (Men) %	1851 (Women) %
January	30	70
February	27	73
March	26	74
April	29	71
May	27	73
June	26	74
July	27	73
August	29	71
September	31	69
October	31	69
November	37	63
December	31	69

That 'dreadful mortality' accelerated its pace from the end of 1845, although no significant increase was evident until February 1846. In 1845 there were 486 deaths, the highest of these in the months January to June, a period of no potato failure (see table 13). The summer months show a much lower rate, due to the reduced rate of admissions and increased rate of discharges for the summer months. The autumnal increases in admissions are indicative of an increased mortality.

It took several months for the famine menace to reveal its physical effects on the human condition. The revelation began in February 1846 with a total of sixty-four deaths, a 37 per cent rise on the previous month. This increase continued until the summer. There was a seasonal reduction in admissions and simultaneously a decline in the mortality figures. Deaths were largely attributable to the typhus fever, which appeared in the spring of 1846.

It seemed at the time that famine conditions had abated and the potato failure was reminiscent of earlier failures that decade, which were short-lived. However speculation proved inaccurate. The blight had infected the crop and the effects of another year of blight in the winter of 1846 and in 1847 would ultimately be more calamitous than the previous year. The crop that appeared so 'luxuriant in July' was by September 'tainted with the odour of decaying potatoes.'

Table No. 13: Monthly mortality figures for 1845–1851

Date	1845	1846	1847	1849	1850	1851
Jan.	43	47	178		110	130
Feb.	52	64	606		120	219
Mar.	55	60	675	164	184	239
Apr.	52	76	523	317	141	176
May	48	88	407	368	156	219
June	42	32	233	255	157	207
July	18	28		130	86	110
Aug.	28	42		106	64	58
Sept.	28	42		90	95	42
Oct.	18	51		48	52	48
Nov.	52	113		48	54	56
Dec.	50	237		83	80	46
Total	**486**	**880**	**2,622**	**1,609**	**1,319**	**550**

Note on table: *There are omissions in the above table of figures for the years 1847 & 1849 because the minutes books for these periods are not available*

Of the salvaged though 'tainted' potatoes, the yield was only enough to feed the population for one month.[19] By November the effects of the second visitation of the blight were evident in terms of mortality. After the first failure in November 1845 the impact on mortality was slight with 52 deaths. In 1846 it was 113. This increase was also affected by rising admissions for that month. However the actual death rate per thousand inmates did increase. In January of 1846, the effects of the first failure were evident with 3.3 deaths per thousand inmates in the house. The death rate had accelerated to 6.6 by November 1846.

In 1846 deaths accounted for 6 per cent of the total admissions of that year. Workhouse conditions contributed to the fatalities when compounded by the contagious diseases brought into the house by each new inmate. In this environment the relief functions of the workhouse were crippled from within. Increased admissions affected mortality but diseases such as epidemic fever, dysentery and continuous exposure to what was at the time thought to be miasmic air advanced death.

Table No.14: Average number of deaths per 1,000 inmates in Cork union work-house for 1846

	Jan. 1846	Mar. 1846	June 1846	Aug. 1846	Nov. 1846
Deaths per 1,000 inmates	3.3	7.3	5	3.2	6.6

If November saw the number of deaths double, then December continued this trend. Figures doubled in a single month from 113 to 237. Subsequently they tripled in February 1847 to over 600. The total number of deaths in 1847 for Cork workhouse cannot be calculated since the minute book for the second half of the year is missing. The catastrophic impact is nonetheless evident, it would ultimately have been much higher that the earlier part of the year, just by the single fact alone that the winter months were always the worst and this year was particularly worse than any of the other years. Between January to June 1847 2,622 deaths were recorded whereas in the entire year of 1846 the death total was 880. The death toll of the famine was by then leaving its mark. One can only imagine the total horror and devastation that must have faced not only the inmates but also the staff and officers of the house on a daily basis. The poor law commissioners' report for 1847 made references to the various experiences of the workhouses in Connaught and the south of Ireland. They were in a 'frightful state of distress and were crowded to an extent far beyond their capacity and that the consequences had been disastrous. The seeds of contagious disease have been introduced and the disease has spread to other inmates and to the officers of the house'.[20]

Who were the victims of Black '47? Continuing the pattern established in previous years, there were greater admissions of females and consequently higher numbers of female deaths. (See figure 7) 1847 was no exception. Female deaths (above the age of fifteen years) totalled 713 and male deaths (above the age of fifteen years) amounted to 571.

The increase in female deaths was higher than 1846, primarily because of the fact that more women were in the workhouse and

Fig. 7: *Male and female mortality for 1845*

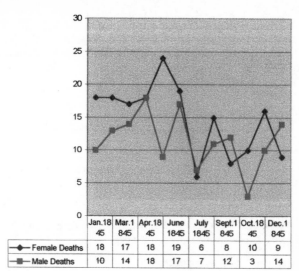

	Jan.18 45	Mar.1 845	Apr.18 45	June 1845	July 1845	Sept.1 845	Oct.18 45	Dec.1 845
Female Deaths	18	17	18	19	6	8	10	9
Male Deaths	10	14	18	17	7	12	3	14

Fig. 8: *Male and female mortality for 1846*

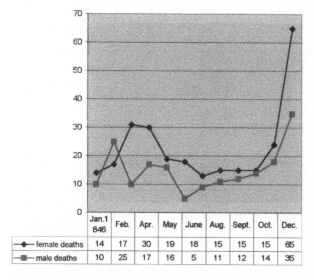

	Jan.1 846	Feb.	Apr.	May	June	Aug.	Sept.	Oct.	Dec.
female deaths	14	17	30	19	18	15	15	15	65
male deaths	10	25	17	16	5	11	12	14	35

that the female sex appeared more susceptible to certain famine illnesses. Secondly, women made up between 65 and 79 per cent of the inmates in Cork union workhouse for the period January to June as outlined in table 15.

Table No.15: Percentage composition of men and women (above fifteen years of age) for 1847

Date	1847 (Men) %	1847 (Women) %
January	35	65
February	25	75
March	25	75
April	21	79
May	25	75
June	26	74

Both the female and male death numbers mirror each other and are suggestive that the same factors influenced both their mortality (see figure 8). These factors notably are the influence of seasonal changes, the workhouse conditions, the timing and effects of disease.

These patterns were still apparent in 1849. In the ten-month period March to December there were 902 adult deaths, a decline on the previous year. Both male and female deaths continued along the lines of those in 1847. Mortality of both sexes increased steadily in the period March to July and thereafter it levelled out. This coincided with the cholera epidemic, then rampant in the house. By August the workhouse was declared free of cholera. As the malign influence of the cholera epidemic abated, mortality figures subsequently reduced and a sense of stability of a sort was observed in the figures.

Table No. 16: Numbers of male and female deaths for March to December 1849

	Mar.	Apr.	May	June	July	Aug.	Sept.	Oct.	Nov.	Dec.
Male deaths	29	131	71	66	25	44	30	15	17	16
Female deaths	29	76	145	65	32	26	26	20	16	23

With total deaths numbering 1,319 in 1850 it became obvious that the workhouse was entering a period of stability. The readjusted house capacity of 4,700 in December 1849 and the normalisation, which occurred in the numbers of recorded deaths in 1850 and 1851, signalled that the famine itself had abated. Left in its stead was a legacy of destruction. The workhouse was more suited to fulfilling its ameliorative function by 1850, although any neglect of sanitation facilities and an increase in admissions could lead to a high mortality in the house at any time.

Exiting the institution took three forms. Inmates either absconded, died or were discharged. Discharge from the house was granted as soon as possible to inmates once their immediate distress was attended to. An expedient discharge system was necessary in order to avoid overcrowding and to provide vacancies for the queues seeking entry. Ideologically, this policy of speedy discharges was essential, as the guardians feared an over reliance on the relief system would lead to increasing idleness among the Irish paupers. Economically, it was believed that efficient house management would be achieved through a policy of cost consciousness, hence the cost per inmate would be reduced if they were discharged more efficiently.

Discharges were not always straightforward and in accordance with the policy of relief. The following categories of inmates were more readily discharged. Inmates who were sick upon admission and being convalescent were once again speedily discharged. Those whose destitution was found to be ill substantiated, those whose desertion was proved false and those who transgressed house rules were punished by immediate discharge. Discharge for inmates meant either their destitution had been sufficiently alleviated or they in some manner procured a punishment that curtailed their relief. Discharge was perceived often as a means of correction.

Discharge figures like those of admission and mortality indicate the impact of the famine in numerical terms. In 1845 a pattern emerged where a higher numbers of females were discharged in comparison to the numbers of males discharged. It became a permanent feature throughout the famine and was substantiated by the greater amount of female admissions. It also emphasised the inadequacies of accommodation as the house capacity constantly overflowed and it illustrated the guardians' determination to provide relief for all that sought it. In 1845 there were 2,446 female discharges as opposed to 1,414 male discharges. Each month of 1845 displayed a higher number of female to male discharges. By 1846 and 1847 the 'great calamity' was underway in the workhouse.[21]

A calamitous change appeared as a doubling of discharge numbers occurred in 1846 in both categories. Female and male discharges amounted to 4,712 and 3,082 respectively, though house capacity remained the same as in 1845 at 2,000 inmates. The sharp rise in the discharge numbers was in line with the increasing admissions in the early quarter of 1846. The latter months were showing the effects of the second potato failure. Increased admissions exacted a pressure on the capacity of the house and induced even speedier discharges. These discharges represented the most populous sectors of the inmate population, notably the female wards. In addition, in November 1846 the pressure of admissions was such that the identity and union of residence of each pauper was queried in an attempt to alleviate the problems of overcrowding. Many paupers had obtained their inmate status without the officials knowing that they came from the countryside. It was policy that each union workhouse was for those resident in the area. Many of the county's destitute made their way to Cork city hoping to seek out a life somewhat better than the life they left. As a result there followed a large exit of paupers who were non-residents of the Cork union. On 7 November 1846 the guardians ratified a decision,

> that all inmates of this union workhouse who are not residents of the Cork union shall be forthwith discharged for the purpose of giving proper and comfortable accommodation to the resident destitute paupers of our own union who have the most natural and legal claim to admission.[22]

Increased admissions led to an increased number of discharges, usually as a means of regulating house capacity. The only exception to that situation was when the annual decline in admissions occurred during the summer months. This time it was not mirrored by a decline in discharge numbers, rather the discharge figures peaked. Inmates sought discharges more frequently in summer as weather conditions were more favourable to life outside the house. Inmates anticipated a better yield of crops in the summer of 1846 and were willing to leave their confinement. This reduced the population of the house to a level in some way capable of accommodating the influx of paupers, which arrived in the autumn of 1846 following the second potato failure. Although still grossly overcrowded, the vicious cycle of admissions and discharges was in some way relieved through the summer discharges.

Summer discharges had little effect upon the unrelenting streams of admissions in 1847. The admissions (of those over fifteen years of age) for 1847 (Jan.–June) totalled 7,817 and the discharges for those above fifteen years were 4,173. By comparison in 1846 the total yearly adult discharges numbered 7,794 and admissions were 15,355. 1847 was much worse than 1846 in all aspects, one can assume that the admissions figures after July would have steadily increased and peaked in the winter months of November and December 1847. 'It was the huge influx of inmates in Black '47 that highlighted the workhouse's position as a band-aid over a gaping wound. Suddenly the Cork union had to accommodate over five thousand people'.[23] The terms of residencies of the inmates within Cork workhouse in 1847 tended to be of a longer duration as evidenced by the increasing admissions together with a decline in the number of discharges in 1847 (Jan.–June). The ratio of admissions to discharges in 1847 (Jan.–June) was 1: 1.8, while in 1846 the ratio was 1: 1.97. This slight decrease suggests, firstly, inmates were slower to request discharge given the total devastation outside the house and secondly, the famine fever and other associated illnesses were prevalent and most inmates required treatment either in the workhouse or the adjoining hospital, consequently prolonging their stay. 1847 continued the patterns of a greater number of female to male discharges with 2,678 and 1,495 respectively being recorded in 1847 (Jan.–June).[24]

Recorded evidence of discharges for 1848 is non-existent as the minute books are missing for this period. However the pressures of overcrowding and the need to discharge inmates was evident in 1848. The Outgoing Letter Book for 1848 details emigration and assisted passage as a means of alleviating these pressures. In February, Mr O'Shaughnessey, then clerk of the union, wrote to the admiral in Cobh outlining that a decision had been taken to 'enter fifty to one hundred young lads at present inmates of the workhouse to her Majesty's Navy.'[25] In May a decision was taken to forward 200 names to the poor law commissioners for assisted passage to Australia.[26]

The number of assisted passages and the construction of auxiliary buildings in the period July 1847 to March 1849 were confirmation of the pressures and problems caused by the overwhelming admissions. It is not inaccurate to assume that the discharges in the period July 1847 to March 1849 were less frequent than in the earlier years of the famine. Many inmates in the early years felt that the famine conditions would be short-lived and characteristic of previous shortages. Many sought to be discharged in anticipation of improving potato yields. This mentality had somewhat evaporated by mid-1847 due to the consecutive failures and meagre resources, which were all consumed by then. People continued to starve and the famine diseases became more virulent during and after 1847.

Though 1849 saw the end of the actual famine, a more alarming issue arose in the form of the cholera epidemic. The cumulative effects of the overcrowding, bodily wastage due to malnutrition and starvation combined with an absence of quick medical treatment for festering diseases, all facilitated the spread of cholera. The need to curtail the cholera epidemic led to an increasing amount of discharges in an attempt to stem the epidemic and purge the disease from the building. Figure 9 illustrates how the pattern of greater female discharge numbers was still dominating. However, the actual trajectory for each category follows a similar route suggesting the discharges for both sexes were influenced by the same factors in 1849.

From March to May 1849 discharges rose steadily in line with the constant flow of admissions and the seasonal adjustment. In

Fig. 9: *Greater number of females to males discharged during period March to December 1849 – the lines graphs incline and decline at similar points.*

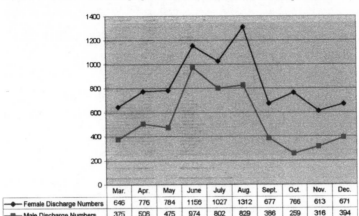

	Mar.	Apr.	May	June	July	Aug.	Sept.	Oct.	Nov.	Dec.
Female Discharge Numbers	646	776	784	1156	1027	1312	677	766	613	671
Male Discharge Numbers	375	506	475	974	802	829	386	259	316	394

May 1849 the workhouse experienced the cholera epidemic. The initial signs of cholera were noted in early May and by late July the master reported that the crisis had lifted. One would assume that the level of discharges would decrease in a cholera epidemic as convalescing fever victims and other inmates would be in receipt of medical attention. This however was not the case. In fact the annual summer increase occurred on a much larger scale. Rising discharges reflected the mounting admissions during the epidemic. It can be argued that many who had not contracted cholera outside the house feared for their lives and were driven inside in the false belief that they would be safer in the workhouse and have some access to medical help. Cholera was a matter of speculation at that time, its advance via contaminated water sources was relatively unknown. The guardians aimed to provide relief and medical attention, but they reduced the period of residency for inmates in an attempt to care for as many victims as possible.

The actual extent of the cholera epidemic is evident in a comparison with the summer period of 1850. By 1850 the famine was over and the legacy of disease and wastage remained. Thus one can assume that the figures represented in the following graph for 1850, would exhibit a certain pattern of normalisation within the house.

Fig. 10: Number of females and males discharged during 1850

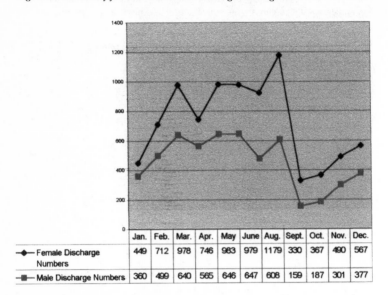

	Jan.	Feb.	Mar.	Apr.	May	June	Aug.	Sept.	Oct.	Nov.	Dec.
—◆— Female Discharge Numbers	449	712	978	746	983	979	1179	330	367	490	567
—■— Male Discharge Numbers	360	499	640	565	646	647	608	159	187	301	377

During the summer of 1850 discharges were higher than the previous months but the increase was not as sharp as that which occurred in 1849 (see figures 9 and 10). This indicates that the cholera epidemic not only increased mortality but also led to a higher incidence of discharges.

From September 1849 the level of discharges was reduced and between June 1850 and December 1851 the worst effects of the famine were over and the resulting drop in discharges became more evident. A period of normalisation had finally returned. The efficacy of the house in dealing with the number of inmates is evident in the stabilisation and reduction in the discharge figures. Even the gulf between the male and female discharges is seen to narrow. It outlines the female composition of the house, although always greater than the male population of the house, was by then in decline. This is evident in the aged/infirm category. Table 17 shows how the female proportion of inmates has dropped from 74–78 per cent in the years 1846–1849 to 52–74 per cent by 1851.

Table No. 17: Percentage composition of aged/infirm men and women in Cork workhouse in 1851

Date	1851 (Men) %	1851 (Women) %
January	48	52
February	35	65
March	34	66
April	37	63
May	34	66
June	34	66
July	31	69
August	29	71
September	28	72
October	28	72
November	29	71
December	26	74

However, this decrease was not evident among the able-bodied category, which remained relatively unchanged in terms of the proportion of able-bodied female inmates. This further corroborates the sociological impact of the famine on the family unit. After the famine there were vast numbers of abandoned and orphaned children, together with many deserted families, i.e. the father had deserted his family, as will be later discussed in detail in chapter four. Meanwhile the percentage composition of able- bodied female inmates remained at a level consistent with famine conditions as evidenced in table 18:

Table No. 18: Percentage composition of able-bodied men and women in Cork workhouse in 1851

Date	1851 (Men) %	1851 (Women) %
January	30	70
February	27	73
March	26	74
April	29	71
May	27	73
June	26	74
July	27	73
August	29	71

September	31	69
October	31	69
November	37	63
December	31	69

These women were the legacy of the famine's sociological impact. For these able-bodied women the workhouse functioned as a surrogate spouse, supporting and ameliorating their destitution while feeding and educating their children.

The very impact of the famine on the role of the workhouse is especially evident by calculating the actual number of famine victims who passed through Cork union workhouse. These starving people were no more than a number to the poor law authorities and it is fitting that they be commemorated through an analysis of their admission, mortality and discharge figures. All the evidence emphasises that the famine adjusted the role of the workhouse. Under the poor law the workhouse facilitated the relief of the destitute. Influenced by the famine the workhouse's role was adjusted to include not only the relief of those assumed destitute but those also whose destitution became more desperate during the famine. The role of the house was one of alleviation of immediate destitution for those seeking admission.

The severity of the famine meant that the aspirations of the guardians often fell victim to their endeavours. In their philanthropic impulses to accommodate as many destitute persons as possible, while extending the house capacity, they were in fact greatly reducing the sanitary facilities and subsequently weakening the position of the workhouse's attempts at relief. As a result the workhouse system functioned as a catalyst for an accelerated march of death through the house. Analyses of the statistics provide insights into the sociological and gender dimensions of the workhouse. They reveal and chart the impact of the famine from 1845 to 1849. By contrasting these figures to those of 1850–51 it becomes apparent that the primary functions of the house to provide relief and to make a difference were slowly returning.

3

Inmate Health

The famine pang and fever pain,
Tear the nation's heart in twain,
Human help is sought in vain.[1]

These lines from a poem entitled 'The Famine Year 1847' penned by a Young Irelander reflect the hardships endured by many during the famine. It is an apt opening to this section dealing with starvation, malnutrition and rampant disease. Famine fever, pain and assistance which in some cases arrived too late or sometimes was 'sought in vain' were all too common afflictions for the workhouse inmate. Any exploration of the fever, disease and medicinal assistance will inevitably lead to a discussion on how the most basic and fundamental aspects of an existence within the confines of Cork workhouse were often contributing factors to the ill-health of inmates. Examining areas such as the inadequate sleeping arrangements, overcrowded accommodation, poor diet, a lack of hygiene and sanitation facilities together with the more serious pathological effects of disease and epidemic tells a gruesome story. When combined with the remedial efforts undertaken (and in some cases not undertaken) by the workhouse health officials, the story becomes more horrific. Any discussions of inmates' health and their general welfare cannot be discussed autonomously, they must be analysed in accordance with the medical and scientific contexts of their era. To fully understand the nature of famine diseases and epidemics it is important to allude to the extent of the medical advances between 1845 and 1852 lest unfounded criticisms be laid upon competent medical staff. It is all too easy to blame the medical officers for not doing enough, especially in hindsight. Given their medical knowledge they often made diagnoses, sometimes accurate and sometimes not. They prescribed what they believed to be the best treatments given the remedies available to them. More often than not their remedies for illness and disease were not enough, but in this they cannot be held culpable.

Inside the institution the health and general welfare of inmates was under the supervision of the workhouse medical staff, which consisted of one physician, one assistant physician, one resident apothecary, nurses and some female inmates who served as nurses' aides. Nurses' aides were classified as voluntary officers of the house and they received additional rations for their endeavours. According to *Croly's Medical Directory* only three of the seventy practising physicians in Cork city were associated with the workhouse in 1846. *Croly's Medical Directory* lists the names, addresses and provides supplementary information on each physician.[2]

Dr O'Connor was appointed the workhouse physician in 1839. He was in receipt of a salary of £70-0s-0d per annum in 1842 which increased to £25-0s-0d per quarter by June 1847.[3] His salary was on a par with that of the master. Residing at South Mall, he was an eminent physician and lectured at Cork School of Medicine in 1846. By 1849 he was teaching at the medical faculty of the newly established Queen's College Cork. Dr O'Connor was assisted by Dr Popham, another expert physician. He resided at Marlborough Street. He also engaged in duties outside of the workhouse, tending to the patients of the North Infirmary hospital and held a lectureship in physiology at Cork School of Medicine. The account books show that in 1847 he earned £20-0s-0d quarterly.[4]

Dr William Stoker Gardiner was the workhouse apothecary and he was given lodgings on site. He was appointed to the position in 1839 on a salary of £30-0s-0d per annum and an additional allowance of £30 rations. His salary also increased by 1847 to £27-10s-0d per quarter. In 1849, a third physician, Dr William Charles Townsend, of Old George's Street, joined the medical staff. The increase in the salaries around 1847 could be seen as being in accordance with the increased demands on the workhouse doctors, so too did the appointment of Dr Townsend highlight the issues of overcrowding within the workhouse. It was essential that the medical team attending to the needs of the house increase from Black '47 onwards to cope with the all too frequent outbreaks of fever and disease.

All physicians in the workhouse were deemed to be competent and expert and held in esteem by their peers. Dr Popham published a series of articles relating to his experiences of fever and climate in the Munster region, as did Dr O'Connor. The health and welfare of the inmates lay in the hands of these physicians and apothecary. They administered relief in a house designed for 2,000 persons and during chronically overcrowded occasions they cared for over 6,000 persons.

Upon admission, paupers were lodged in probationary wards, which were located adjacent to the physician's office. Not solely for hygienic reasons but also for reasons of deterrence they were de-loused, cleansed communally and kitted out in the workhouse uniform before being directed to their dormitories. Dormitory conditions illustrated the cramped and congested conditions even before 1845.

Spatial arrangements for dormitories were an ingenious invention of the architect, Wilkinson. Although cramped and basic they fulfilled their function of affording a maximum number of persons accommodation in the workhouse. He provided bedsteads only for the aged and infirm men and women on the ground floor. Regarding the able-bodied adults and children he proposed 'an arrangement which will combine cleanliness and convenience with comfort'.[5] His proposals involved the construction of a continuous bedstead or a raised platform eight inches above floor level along each side of the room, thus forming a gangway. Straw mattresses piled six inches thick and three feet six inches wide were intended to accommodate two persons and each was given one blanket.

As a result each pauper occupied approximately about two feet of space and each room accommodated approximately forty-eight persons or 200 persons in terms of the upper floors and 500 on the ground floor. The congested conditions and foul atmosphere of these rooms can be easily detected where by the complete absence of closets and the presence of two large urine tubs in each of the wards, which frequently overflowed, and the planks of the flooring had to be often renewed.[6] These were typical of accommodation arrangements throughout the country and were equally evident in Cork workhouse in 1840.

During 1840, the first fully operational year of Cork workhouse, the *Southern Reporter* revealed that the house had capacity for more inmates since two persons did not occupy each bed.[7] In March 1840 an assessment of available accommodation highlighted the following: 321 able-bodied women occupied 164 beds, (i.e. 1.9 persons per bed), 51 nurses and their 49 infants had 56 beds (i.e. 1.7 persons per bed). It was proposed that these two categories could accommodate an extra 50 persons whilst the 171 aged and infirm women occupied 108 beds (i.e. 1.5 persons per bed) and could accommodate a further 45 persons. Meanwhile girls under thirteen years slept three in a bed.[8] Likewise the minutes of April 1840 refer to the state of the flooring. The house management committee in April 1840 chastised the guardians for admitting paupers who were 'not totally destitute' and for incurring additional expenses much of which was attributable to furniture 'such as the new bed flooring which was very roughly planned'.[9] The committee did however acknowledge that the new workhouse should have durable deal flooring. They were particularly infuriated that repair costs to the temporary house were to be discharged by the costs of the new house and that the repairs were unnecessary being 'only for a short while'.[10] During the period 1845–51 accommodation came under increasing pressure.

The blight of September 1845 rendered the potato crop useless and admissions to the workhouse increased. Inmates were subjected to increasing congestion but these conditions did not become so severe as to create a radical change in arrangements until early 1846. In February, Richard Dowden, chairman of the board of guardians, wrote to the poor law commissioners stressing that 'the influx of paupers is so great that their admission is on account of their utter destitution, that this house contains on this day [21 Feb.] 480 more than it was built to accommodate'.[11] Dowden warned a figure of 480 above the capacity of 2,000 was detrimental to the welfare of the inmates.

In the ensuing months such guidelines were largely ignored as the levels of overcrowding escalated. The strain on accommodation resources was especially evident in April 1846 when the 'lunatics' and 'idiots' were deemed to require too much space. Space apportioned for nine lunatics could provide accommodation for at least fifty 'destitute applicants'. Richard Dowden petitioned the commissioners to remove such lunatics to the lunatic asylum. Dowden was of the opinion that lunatics did not belong in the workhouse but in 'another competent institution'. Recognising the limitations of his remit as chairman he noted that 'it is not in our power, therefore we earnestly request that you will please apply to the Lord Chancellor'.[12] The result was favourable as the commissioners were 'of the opinion that the Lunatic Asylum be compelled to receive patients from the workhouse and the cost to be discharged through the poor rate.'[13] Meanwhile the spatial arrangements of the lunatics were reduced. Idiots and lunatics appear to have been treated in an inferior manner in comparison to the regular paupers clamouring for admission.

The same week the guardians resolved that they 'should have the privilege of giving, provisionally, admission tickets to any destitute poor person to be admitted until examined before the board'.[14] This policy of provisional admission was criticised as a means of adding to the problem of overcrowding and it highlighted the fact that many of those seeking admission were not residents of the union but were vagrants and all too often from other union districts.

By August 1846 the guardians presented their concerns on overcrowding to the commissioners:

> Probably you are not aware that the Cork workhouse contains more than the generality of country houses, numbers more inmates than either of the Dublin houses and that the duties of the Cork house are immeasurably greater than those of the Dublin houses when combined ... I need only observe that the united admissions or discharges of those of Dublin do not exceed 100 weekly whereas in Cork they amount frequently to over 300 weekly.[15]

To strengthen their case, the staff inferred that their grievances, notably those of underpayment and insufficient staff numbers were prejudicial to the provision of an adequate inmate health system, 'and yet it is strange to say that the staff of these [Dublin] houses exceeds that of Cork by 40 per cent and on the point of salary by nearly £400 in the aggregate.'[16]

Despite their grievances, having being moved by the suffering they witnessed the staff often performed acts of humanity and care. One philanthropic impulse amongst the workhouse staff was clearly demonstrated in the last week of September 1846. Unable to cope with the increasing numbers of paupers seeking admission; the master provided breakfast for 11,633, in addition to the actual workhouse inmates.[17] The poor law commissioners believed this practice to be objectionable. They declared the use of union funds on such an exercise as illegal. 'This system of giving breakfast at the door is contrary to law … without precedent in Ireland or in England and it is fraught with the probability of evil consequences to the moral condition of the labouring classes.'[18] However, funds were not diverted to the relief of those already in the workhouse. Workhouse provisions lists indicated that basic necessities such as rugs and blankets were in short supply. One Cork historian evokes the horrors of overcrowding, 'bedding often consisted of dirty straw; without even a blanket in sight and as many as six persons underneath one rug. The lack of sanitation made these hovels no better than rat-infested pits.'[19]

Overcrowding was the primary complaint of the guardians in the minutes during 1846 and 1847. These cramped conditions are extensively recorded in the minutes books for the period November 1845 to August 1846. By April 1846 the number of inmates exceeded capacity by 701 and it reached its peak in February 1847 with 5,310 inmates. By erecting temporary sheds and converting rooms such as the female surgical ward into dormitories, capacity was increased by 800 to 2,800. Such alterations, despite offering the possibility of respite from overcrowding, were in the main pre-judicial to the welfare of inmates as it reduced the efficiency of the house medical facilities which were already under severe stress. It was not until March 1850 that the number of inmates came close to equalling the amount of available accommodation. During 1845–50 overcrowding was excessive, yet the demand for accommodation meant there would be a reduction in facilities elsewhere in the house, thus aiding and abetting the spread of fever and disease.

In this season of scarcity the immune systems of the paupers were diminished. Their inadequate nutritional intake assisted the spread of fever and disease reached epidemic proportions throughout the house. Commentators of pre-famine economic history have drawn attention to the 'contrast between the abject poverty of the masses and their relatively high nutritional status'.[20] The variety of potato most commonly cultivated in pre-famine Ireland was the lumper. Introduced from Scotland in the early 1800s, its popularity amongst the tenant farmers stemmed from its ease of cultivation and its abundant yields, adaptability to poor soils and most importantly – its reliability. According to Ó Grada it proved to be 'doubly notorious'. It was 'the poor food in the decades leading up to the famine and for offering such poor resistance to phythopthera infestans, fair enough, although the Lumper was definitely dull fare it usually provided the requisite calories before 1845'.[21] Previous potato failures and diminished yields occurred and the effects of the blight of September 1845 were perceived as yet another 'season of scarcity'.[22] Inaccurate in their prediction, the diet of the Irish paupers was altered. This was reflected in the alterations made to the workhouse diet during 1845 to 1846.

Entries in the union minutes provide very exact and comprehensive details of dietaries and the provisions lists. In many cases there are detailed descriptions of the food served, the preparation and the culinary processes. Many of the culinary processes show how a minimum of food was used to feed a maximum of mouths. To understand why diet was so influential upon the health and wellbeing of the inmates it is necessary to assess its nutritional merits and the quantities in which food was provided. It is essential to explore the certain types of food which were selected as workhouse fare.

An examination of the workhouse diet outlines the relationship between one's susceptibility to disease and illness with the acceleration in the spread of disease, often through contaminated foodstuffs. In the creation of a workhouse dietary the administrators had to fulfil two conditions, both of which encapsulated the essence of the Poor Law Act of 1838. Firstly, administrators had to ensure that inmates had enough food to survive. Secondly, the diet had to be sufficiently unattractive as it was assumed that 'a plentiful diet would attract new inmates into the institution'.[23] It thereby strengthened one of the main roles of the workhouse, which was to act as a deterrent to potential admissions.

What the poor law did not count on was the arrival of the famine and in famine years the dietary policies of the workhouses offered a glimmer of hope in what was becoming a deadly fight for survival. Outside the confines of the workhouse access to food depots, currency for purchases and public works schemes were not viable options for all. On one occasion the guardians were accused of contributing to the number of deaths by starvation, due to their delayed payment for work completed under the board of works scheme. Paupers realised that life inside the workhouse could not be much worse than their individual deprivations. Thus the workhouse became the place of last resort.

Workhouse dietary was outlined by the central poor law administrators. At ground level the workhouse physician supervised the dietary arrangements and could make recommendations and substitutions providing that all such suggestions were within the union budget. From 1840, Drs O'Connor and Popham supervised the workhouse dietary. Inmates received their meals at regular times but these were seasonally adjusted. In winter they dined at 8 a.m., 2 p.m. and 6 p.m. and in the summer months breakfast was served at 7 a.m.[24] The main foodstuffs that constituted the workhouse diet were potatoes, oatmeal, bread, milk and tea. By comparison the Northwich union workhouse diet in England included buttermilk, broth, gruel, cooked meat, butter and sugar.[25] Nursing women were allowed the same quantities as able-bodied men and the medical officer arranged the diet for the sick at his own discretion. The latter also applied to Irish workhouses. The discrepancy in the scale of dietary between the Irish and the English paupers is explained by the difference in the type of pauper then common in Ireland. In both institutions the destitute rule was observed but the Irish pauper had a lower level of subsistence and was more heavily reliant on potatoes.

The typical Irish pauper received an adequate energy/calorie intake from his diet consisting largely of potatoes, consuming between five and fourteen pounds of potatoes per day.

Table No.19: Consumption of potatoes by paupers[26]

Potato Consumption	Per day (kgs)	(lbs)
Adult Male	6.4	14
Adult Female	5.1	11.2
Children 11 to 15 yrs.	5.1	11.2
Children under 11 yrs.	2.2	4.9

The high nutritional status of potatoes prevented many of the illnesses common amongst the poor in other countries, especially scurvy and pellagra. The symptoms of scurvy included sponginess and bleeding of the gums and the main cause was a deficiency in vitamin C, whilst pellagra, attributed to a lack of vitamin A, manifested itself in shrivelled skin and bodily wastage. Both were illnesses which were uncommon amongst the Irish pauper class. The reason for this lay in the benefits attributed to a potato diet.

Potato starch is easily digested and gives a slow release of energy. When consumed in copious quantities it provides a sufficient source of protein which contains a small amount of a particularly high quality protein. If the skins are eaten, then their content of fibre more than doubles. Table 20 outlines the nutritional values of one kilogram of potatoes (approximately two pounds).

From these tables, the adult male consumed an average of fourteen pounds per day. This was equivalent to consuming approximately 2,401 calories – a healthy amount. Thus, the relatively 'good' health of the Irish pauper prior to the famine may be explained.

Table No. 20: The nutritional value of boiled potatoes (per kg.)[27]

Energy Value (Kj)	343
Complex Carbohydrate (g.)	19.7
Protein (g.)	1.4
Fat	Trace
Vitamin C (mg.)	4–14
Dietary Fibre (g.)	10

The staples of the diet in 1842 at Cork workhouse reflect the usual diet of the pauper class. Able-bodied inmates received only seven pounds of potatoes daily, this was substituted by bread and oatmeal which were made into a thick porridge. With the onslaught of the 'potato murrain'[28] in 1845 the question being asked was 'where will Ireland be in the event of a universal potato rot?'[29]

In such an eventuality workhouse diets would be altered, the digestive systems of the Irish pauper class would need re-adjustment to other foodstuffs and diseases previously rare would become increasingly prevalent while obtaining an equally nutritious and relatively cheap alternative to potatoes would be problematical. In September 1845 'the murrain' affected potato yields yet it was not so severe as to cause radical changes in the workhouse diet until early 1846. By then reserves were exhausted and the effects of starvation were taking hold. The consecutive failure of the crop emphasised that the dreaded 'universal potato rot had arrived'. Ryan Purcell of the earl of Bandon's estate described the inferior quality of the potato crop, 'the potatoes being so putrefied and rotten that the pig refused to eat them'.[30] The potato ceased to be a viable diet option and on 11 October the master reported that the 'potatoes supplied to this union partake of the prevalent disease and therefore are very wasteful'.[31] This posed two problems for the guardians, firstly it was wasteful and did not adhere to their policy of workhouse economy and secondly, could an economical and substantial dietary replacement be found for potatoes?

Those potatoes that did exist were used in ingenious ways to maximise their food output and reduce economic loss. As a remedy the guardians appointed a house committee to investigate the viability of the 'manufacture of farina by the paupers of the

Fig. 11: Scale of diet to be given to the inmates

BREAKFAST:	DINNER:	SUPPER:

ABLE-BODIED MEN AND WOMEN ABOVE 13 YEARS

BREAKFAST:	DINNER:	SUPPER:
3lbs of potatoes,	3^1/$_2$ lbs of potatoes	6oz of bread
^{1}/$_2$ pint of milk (4 days)	and 1pint of milk	
7oz of oatmeal, ^{1}/$_2$ pint		
of milk (3 days)		

AGED AND THE INFIRM MEN AND WOMEN

BREAKFAST:	DINNER:	SUPPER:
10 oz of bread	2^1/$_2$ lbs of potatoes	6oz of bread
and ^{1}/$_2$ pint of milk	and 1 pint of milk	

CHILDREN ABOVE 5 YEARS AND UNDER 13 YEARS OF AGE

BREAKFAST:	DINNER:	SUPPER:
4oz oatmeal	2^1/$_2$ lbs of potatoes	6oz of bread
and ^{1}/$_2$ pint of milk (3 days)	and ^{1}/$_2$ pint of milk	
2lbs of potatoes, ^{1}/$_2$ pint		
of milk(4 days)		

CHILDREN FROM 2 TO 5 YEARS OF AGE

BREAKFAST:	DINNER:	SUPPER:
6oz of bread	2lbs of potatoes	4oz of bread
and ^{1}/$_2$ pint of milk	and ^{1}/$_2$ pint of milk	

Source: Minute book, 4 April 1842

establishment from the diseased portion of the potatoes'.[32] In November the committee presented its findings. They recommended 'kiln drying of the potatoes and thereby converting them into biscuit'.[33] Kilns were installed though they were of little benefit once the potato reserves were exhausted. Extra rations of bread were introduced on the recommendation of Dr O'Connor as a substitute for potatoes in the diet. The able-bodied received an extra six ounces of bread whilst the aged and infirm received an additional pound of potatoes for dinner and children received a pound of potatoes for breakfast. It was envisaged that extra rations be given to the aged and infirm and the younger inmates in an attempt to compensate them for their dietary deficiencies. It was believed that these two groupings were more susceptible to illness and were less inclined to adapt to the absence of potatoes.

By April 1846 inmates had no choice but to adapt to other foodstuffs. Potatoes were essentially off the menu. Physicians proposed that bread be substituted at dinner and oatmeal at break-fast'.[34] The guardians extended the bakery department and in-creased the numbers of inmates employed there. Even at this time of crisis the workhouse upheld the poor law belief in advancing self-sufficiency. Correspondence from Sir Charles Edward Tre-velyan, assistant secretary of the treasury, to Sir Randolph Routh, of the commissariat branch of the army, who helped organise and administer relief operations in February 1846 outlined that 'per-manent advantages will accrue to Ireland from the scarcity and the measures taken for its relief ... people could be taught to de-pend on themselves for developing the resources of the country, instead of having recourse to the assistance of the government on every occasion.'[35]

These dietary arrangements were enforced for the remainder of the famine period, being only amended by an increase or a de-crease in rations where the budget so allowed or on the house doctor's recommendations. Such dietary considerations are il-lustrated by examining the workhouse provision lists (a sort of shop-ping list which was agreed each Saturday and entered in the minute books) and the costs associated with maintaining the inmates of the union. An assessment of the financial aspects of the dietary arrangements, an exploration of the nutritional value of the diet and the benefits of the diet to the inmates is necessary to get a comprehensive view of the workhouse lifestyle for the Cork union inmate and of his level of health.

An economical yet wholesome diet was the guardians' pri-mary concern. Indian meal became the main substitute for the potato. It gained a somewhat supernatural reputation amongst the Irish paupers. One landlord commented on the myth associated with the meal as follows:

> At the first stage of their proceedings the relief committees were much impeded by the unfounded prejudices which came against it ... To be engendered in the minds of the poor against the use of Indian meal, which would have the effect of turning those who used it – black. I have personal recollections of this prejudice but with time it passed off, they too became eager to avail of the wholesome, economical food thus provided for their relief.[36]

Commentators on nineteenth-century peasants allude to their supernatural beliefs. Another commentator, E. Estyn Evans, proposes that a sense of kinship existed between the peasant and the natural world in areas where tradition was strong, hence, 'sickness and famine of any kind was not only a misfortune but a disgrace, a sign that luck had forsaken one and the evil forces were working against one, the supernatural world was always present'.[37] Accordingly such 'sympathetic magic' often offered the best explanations for many of the tenacious beliefs and practices amongst the Irish peasant.[38] The myth regarding Indian meal perhaps alludes to their inherent distrust of British policies. The belief that the meal turned its victims a 'black' colour has some semblance of truth. It did cause some who ate it to become very ill if the 'meal' was inadequately prepared. Without thorough soaking and boiling it frequently punctured the lining of the stomach. In the absence of potatoes it became the replacement foodstuff.

Inmates received one pound of meal for dinner. Once cooked it accrued to a weight of four pounds. In its quantity and bulk it filled the inmates much the same as potatoes, but it did not have a comparable nutritional status. Its economic value was its most favourable aspect for the guardians. They tendered for cheaper suppliers of Indian meal. On 8 November 1845 they required one tonne, for 1,856 inmates, and by January 1846 they advertised for three tonnes when inmates increased to 2,428.[39] In the later years of 1849–50 the highest order of Indian meal was for four tonnes coinciding with the highest order for ten tonnes of oatmeal which occurred in July and August 1849.[40] By then the inmate population had climbed to 6,805 but was reduced in the following months. By 1850 the inmate population was 4,700. Changes in the quantities of these two dietary commodities of Indian meal and oatmeal reflect the increasing inmate population of the house.

The provision lists of the house provide an insight into the impact of the famine on the health and welfare of inmates. They record the manner in which the famine impeded the availability of other foodstuffs and show that union finances were stretched, the rate was then proving to be increasingly inadequate under such conditions. Any inclusion of meat in the inmate diet was limited. The minutes of 8 November 1845 describe an order for 160$\frac{1}{4}$ lbs of meat to feed 1,856 inmates. This allowed for approximately 1.4 ounces of meat per inmate. However, meat was not distributed as cooked meat, but rather beef heads were used as ingredients in the broth given to the inmates. The only time cooked meat was sanctioned as a main meal was in December 1845 when the guardians announced that 'during this season of good-will, it was resolved to give the paupers a meat diet on Christmas Day.'[41]

By March 1849 it appears that the good will of 1845 had evaporated under the stress of the famine and this became most apparent in the reduced nutritional value of the broth. The quantity of beef heads used in the culinary processes was reduced and a less concentrated broth was provided to the inmates. This is evident from an examination of the provision lists in 1849. Meat in the quantity of 340 lbs was required in March to feed an inmate population three times that of 1845. If meat was to be added to the diet in the same quantities as 1845 the storekeeper should have ordered at least 544 lbs, thus suggesting that financial considerations were in place to the detriment of the health of inmates. Given the limitations of the house budget it is necessary to state that the guardians aimed to provide remedial assistance, albeit meagre, for as many as possible.

In an effort to practice good housekeeping, butter was removed from the diet and was substituted by lard in quantities varying from forty to eighty pounds. Eighty pounds was ordered on 3 November 1849.[42] Fiscal restraint in the maintenance of paupers can be partially attributed to the political changes at this time. Direct supremacy of the British poor law commissioners ended and the control of the Irish poor law was handed over to an executive of Irish commissioners. Previously, the costs of maintaining paupers were acquired half from the poor rate and half from advances by the government. Thus, when the Irish executive took control of the administration of relief, its inherent lack of strict financial scrutiny became obvious.

Fiscal restraint is apparent from an examination of the costs of maintaining paupers from the table below.

Table No. 21: Inmate maintenance cost, 1849–1850[43]

Workhouse: *average cost of maintaining an inmate per week*
Infirmary: *average cost of maintaining a patient per week*
Fever hospital: *average cost of maintaining a fever patient per week*
Provisions: *weekly cost of house provisions and necessaries*

Date	Workhouse	Infirmary	Fever Hospital	Provisions
2 June '49	£0-1s-2³/4d	£0-1s-5¹/8d	£0-1s-10³/4d	£433-14s-9¹/2d
7 July	£0-1s-2¹/2d	£0-1s-4d	£0-1s-9³/4d	£435-4s-7¹/4d
4 August	£0-1s-2¹/4d	£0-1s-6¹/8d	£0-1s-9d	£331-2s-1¹/4d
1 Sept.	£0-1s-1³/4d	£0-1s-4¹/2d	£0-1s-5¹/2d	£253-4s-3¹/4d
6 Oct.	£0-1s- 1³/4d	£0-1s-2³/4d	£0-1s-10¹/2d	£213-11s-6¹/4d
3 Nov.	£0-1s-2d	£0-1s-4¹/4d	£0-1s-10¹/2d	£283-18s-1¹/4d
1 Dec.	£0-1s-1d	£0-0s-11³/4d	£0-1s-4¹/2d	£228-1s-9d
29 Dec.	£0-1s-0d	£0-1s-1d	£0-1s-5d	£271-14s-9¹/4d
5 Jan.'50	£0-0s-11³/4d	£0-1s-1¹/8d	£0-1s-5d	£245-12s-4d

From March 1849 onwards the costs of maintaining paupers in the workhouse and its adjoining general infirmary and fever hospital were reduced. One factor for the reduced expenditure can be attributed to the decline in inmate numbers by December 1849. Auxiliary buildings were demolished and the overall capacity was reduced by 2,400 from August to December when inmates numbered 4,770 and the house was capable of holding 4,700 inmates. The reduction in the overall cost of provisions is normal allowing for the reduction in the number of inmates. However, the cost per inmate should remain steadfast if rations and medical care afforded to inmates were to be of a similar quantity and quality as previously. Proportionality appears to be absent from the financial figures apportioned to the costs of maintaining the inmates.

This unbalanced scenario is further evident by a comparison of the figures for 1845–46. The overall weekly cost for maintaining an average of 2,400 inmates in December to January 1846 was £163 whereas for the same period in 1849–50 amounted to £245.

This appears to be out of proportion in relation to the maintenance costs required for an inmate population of almost 5,000. An approximation based on the earlier figures suggests that the cost should accrue to £417. This shows that there was a shortfall in terms of expenditure on the health and welfare of inmates during the latter years.

A shortfall in this area indicates increased expenses elsewhere in the institution other than the workhouse, infirmary or the fever hospital. More costs were being incurred in areas such as burials. The Cork union ledger account books highlight augmented burial costs and this was apparent in the increased funeral necessities ordered since 1847.[44] In May 1849 (during the cholera epidemic) one thousand yards of flannel was required for shrouding of bodies, 150 deal planks for coffins and an additional 150 barrels of lime for interring the dead.[45] The prevalence of disease imposed further expenses on the management of the house. A new dietary proposal was sent to the guardians in February 1849 placing greater emphasis on Indian meal and advocating economical soup and milk and brown bread.[46]

Bread and milk were always staples in dietary considerations and appear not to have been influenced by fiscal restraint policies. Rather both milk and bread provisions always increased or decreased in accordance with the fluctuations of the inmate population and the amounts given to inmates were unvarying. From December 1845 to June 1846 the weekly quantity of bread increased from 12,000 to 20,000 pounds coinciding with increased admissions. With the usual seasonal decrease in summer admissions, the quantity of bread ordered was reduced to between 16,000 and 18,000 pounds per week. After 1847 bread, the main source of carbohydrate, was reduced with increased reliance on oatmeal and Indian meal.

The calcium requirements of inmates were accommodated through the provision of milk. As with bread, the quantity of milk consumed per week recorded the vagaries of the inmate population. During the period of December 1845 to June 1846 milk consumption increased from 2,484 to 3,520$\frac{1}{2}$ gallons weekly.

Fig. 12: Average bread and milk consumption per inmate, November 1845 to April 1846

Milk	Date	Gallons Consumed	No. of Inmates	Pints per inmate (per day)	
	8 Nov. 1845	2,484	1,856	2.24	
	27 Dec.	2,776	2,041	2.28	
	21 Feb. 1846	3,282	2,442	2.25	
	4 Apr.	3,560	2,633	2.27	
	11 Apr.	3,582$^{1}/_{2}$	2,578	2.33	
	18 Apr.	3,520$^{1}/_{2}$	2.622	2.25	

Bread	Date	Pounds Consumed	No. of Inmates	Amount per inmate (per week)	Amount per inmate (per day)
	8 Nov.1845	12,000	1,856	6.46 lbs	0.93 lbs
	18 Apr. 1846	20,000	2,622	7.62 lbs	1.08 lbs

Source: Calculated from minute book entries, BG 69A5

During the cholera epidemic of 1849 the storekeeper noted that 5,623 gallons were required. Calculated from the inmate returns and the provision lists each inmate received an average of 2.2 pints of milk thereby verifying Cooke and Scanlon's claim that each inmate received two pints of milk daily.[47] Milk, though nutritious and a source of calcium for the inmate, had some negative effects on their health. With such copious quantities being delivered daily to the workhouse the issue of maintaining freshness and heat treatment of the milk was often recorded in the minutes. On one occasion, the doctors claimed the state of the milk was 'prejudicial to the health of inmates' as 'the skim-milk through boiling on its delivery, an hour afterwards becomes sour and turns into curds and whey'.[48] Using skimmed-milk also reduced the vitamin A content available to inmates.

If the state of the milk posed a threat to the wellbeing of inmates, so too did bacteria lurking undetected (and relatively unknown to the medical community at that time) in the milk. Bacteria was transmitted by flies and as such milk became an innocent, though none-the-less, causative agent in the spread for example of ophthalmic diseases. In the mid-1800s the causal links of ill-health to food and accommodation arrangements were not of the utmost importance as the transmission of disease at the time was speculative. One physician of the house of industry in 1830 did acknowledge the link between congested living arrangements and illness whereby 'giving them medicine or anything else while they are put up in crowded wards as to the children they were actually dying from the want of good evil.'[49] During 1845–51 the more pathological effects of disease and fever escalated as a consequence of the severe overcrowding, low resistance to disease and a reduced nutritional intake. In these conditions the workhouse harboured much illness for inmates and often the early symptoms of various diseases were cloaked in the guise of having the appearance of other basic ailments.

Such hidden symptoms become apparent when one examines the descriptions of pauper disabilities and the observations of the paupers at admission. Each pauper's condition and general appearance was recorded in the indoor register. The indoor registers of the Cork union are not extant but they exist in a number of fragments. The following list catalogues the observations contained in the fragments:

Table No. 22: Observations of inmates listed in the indoor register

Able-bodied	Decrepit	Hip-dislocated	On crutches
Apoplectic	Delicate health	Hunchbacked	Paralysis
Asthmatic	Disease of the head	Hurt neck	Pregnant
Bad cough	Dropsy/edema	Idiotic	Rupture
Bad stomach	Dysentery	Infirm	Rheumatism
Consumption	Epileptic	Influenza	Swollen joints
Convalescent	Erysipelas	Itch	Sore eyes
Crippled	Fractured thigh	Lame	Sore throats
Dead leg	Hard of hearing	Liver complaint	Ulcer on face
Dead hand	Healthy	Nearly blind	Very weak
Deaf and dumb	Helpless (old age)	Nervous	Weak intellect

Source: Indoor registers, BG65 GI, G5, BG69 G5

Although these descriptions appeared to be minor afflictions, many progressed into more serious diseases and were too often fatal. The following list provides a list of diseases diagnosed amongst inmates during the famine:

Fig. No. 13: Medical diseases and conditions within the Cork union workhouse during the famine years

Cholera	Edema (Dropsy)	Scurvy	Typhus	Dysentery	Boils
Apoplexy	Conjunctivitis (Opthalamia)	Epilepsy	Rickettsia	Gout	Bursitis
Asthma	Rheumatism	Myositis	Relapsing Fever	Pellagra	Endo-carditis
Idiot 'savant'	Tuberculosis (Consumption)	Erysipelas	Staphylococcus Bacterium	Malnutrition	Hantaviruses (Rodents)

The immediate effect of the first partial crop failure of 1845 saw an increase in the numbers of undernourished paupers but the ability of the human body to adapt fairly well to a reduction in the intake of nutrients meant that diseases did not reach epidemic proportions until 1846. Cutting the intake by half will reduce one's body weight by one-quarter. However, an individual may subsist at this level for almost six months without suffering any adverse health effects. The second crop failure in 1846 resulted in a further reduction in nutritional intake and more serious diseases then took their toll on the pauper host in the workhouse.

As stated earlier a deficiency in both vitamin A and vitamin C causes pellagra and scurvy respectively. Scurvy was relatively unknown in pre-famine Ireland. According to the workhouse physician, Dr Popham, the only cases he knew of were amongst 'sailors of guano vessels, the continued exposure to the vapour of ammonia appearing to act as a determining cause'.[50] He could assign no cause to the appearance of scurvy on land. Popham's view underlines the primitive and speculative nature of mid-eighteenth-century medicine as regards bacteriology and the causative agents of infections. He stated that scurvy was a frequent scourge in the workhouse attacking the female inmates with more frequency than the males, 'moreover individuals in the prime of life'.[51] Hence scurvy and pellagra would have been undetected upon admission given their rarity. However some descriptions in the indoor registers could be indicative of the early stages of scurvy, such as painful swollen limbs and skin discolouration. McArthur notes the latter stages of scurvy, where 'massive effusions of blood under the skin [occur] causing tension and great pain'.[52]

Swollen, stiff, painful limbs, joints and skin changes were indicative of other diseases such as xerophthalamia, dropsy/edema and rheumatic conditions such as gout, ostheoarithitis. Xerophthalamia, a dryness and thickening of the surface of the eye, is caused by deficiency in vitamin A and left untreated caused blindness. Bacteria-carrying flies transmitted other ophthalmic diseases. Exposed milk was a notorious source for transmitting such diseases especially to the children. This disease was further accentuated when skimmed milk or buttermilk were provided instead of whole milk, as both have significantly reduced levels of vitamin A, iron, and protein.

Famine dropsy or edema manifested itself as swellings in the lower parts of the body and limbs following the accumulation of excess fluid in the body organs, muscles and tissues. Again the registers illustrate such symptoms. Caused by low blood protein after starvation, it frequently became associated with the onset of fever attacks. Thus the abject starvation of the famine victims nurtured many an epidemic.[53]

Robins notes that there was widespread recognition that human squalor and abysmally low standards of hygiene facilitated the spread of disease.[54] The conditions in the workhouse were unsanitary. The minutes frequently refer to the overflowing cess-pit. According to the workhouse physician there was a 'lack of personal cleanliness and the effluvia accumulated from such numbers herding together like gregarious animals' led to an onslaught of bacterial and louse transmitted infections such as erysipelas, endocarditis, dysentery, typhus fever and relapsing fever.[55]

Erysipelas is a bacterial skin infection transmitted through open wounds and often becomes epidemic. The presence of erysipelas is easily detected through characteristic red butterfly-shaped patches on the face. It was common in the workhouse amongst the older adults and children, especially newborn infants whose umbilical stumps were susceptible to the streptococci bacteria. Dr Popham reported that erysipelas was increasingly prevalent, 'erysipelas of the head and face, rheumatism abscesses with extensive matter borrowing over the cartilage of the ribs'.[56] Malnutrition contributed to its spread in addition to the open sewers and cess pools which were in close proximity to the house.

Bacteria of the genus *Staphyloccus* was responsible for the acute infections.[57] Two types of staphylocci exist, *staphylococcus aureus* and *staphylococcus epidermis*. Commonly found in air, water, skin and the upper pharynx, staphylococcus has a parasitic function. Descriptions of inmates with weak hearts, boils, liver complaints and throat infections are common. These were primary infections but when left untreated developed into more serious and fatal infections. *Staphylococcus aureus* can lead to acute infection and inflammation of the heart called endocarditis, the initial infection being usually an infection of the teeth, tonsils or sinuses. *Staphylococcus epidermis* occurs universally on the skin. It can take advantage of a suppressed immune system and can aggravate a pre-existing condition. Given the hazards of overcrowding and inadequate sanitation arrangements, especially the communal bathing facilities it can be presumed that much of the wounds, boils, carbuncles, liver and kidney complaints may be attributed to the increased presence of such bacteria.

The workhouse system was devised to deal with destitution and not disease. Invariably special fever accommodation in the workhouse was not available. There was insufficient room to isolate many of the fever patients. 'It became impossible to separate all the sick from the well'.[58] Cork workhouse propagated fever outbreaks by providing the necessary breeding conditions. Corrigan in his paper on famine and fever acknowledged that dysentery, typhus and relapsing fever accompanied the famine:

> No sooner was famine felt from the deficient crop than pestilence followed raging with great violence through the country … fever following famine as closely as effect can follow cause, in every instance the appearance and prevalence of one is the indication of the commencement of the other.[59]

From November 1845 there was an increased incidence of dysentery, typhus fever and relapsing fever amongst the inmates. Dysentery, known as 'the bloody flux', is bacillary in origin and is spread by direct contact or consumption of contaminated water, milk or food. Flies carrying bacteria on their feet can transmit it. The bacilli produce inflammation and ulceration of the intestines causing violent diarrhoea. Popham believed that 'the dietary of workhouses has certainly a tendency to promote the disease'.[60]

At Cork workhouse dysentery occurred in tandem with famine fever which is also known as typhoid fever. Two types of typhoid fever were observed in the workhouse, typhus and relapsing fever. Typhus was always common but relapsing fever emerged on a greater scale during the famine. Both are transmitted in a similar mode, through *Rickettsia Prowazeki*, micro-organisms carried by the human louse.[61] Typhus, which can be contracted through open wounds or inhalation, was more infectious. Popham's report on epidemic fever in Munster cites an example of contraction of the disease through inhalation when,

> … in the board room of the workhouse three of the guardians were stricken with fever on the same day, and it was afterwards observed that they sat at a particular side of the room in a draught of air which perhaps conveyed the concentrated effluvia from a crowd of paupers waiting in the confined ante-chamber for admission, no case occurred in any other part of the room.[62]

The early symptoms usually appear after ten days after a bite by the louse in the form of rash, itch, fever and mental confusion. Such symptoms were recorded in the inmate descriptions upon admission. Many inmates were listed as being 'nervous', had a 'disease of the head' or were 'insane'. Perhaps the mental confusion was a delirious state occurring from famine fever. The prevalence of typhus may be verified by observations of itch and other words associated with insanity.

Relapsing fever was less virulent and transmitted by body lice and ticks. It occurs in areas of poor hygiene and malnutrition. Symptoms included jaundice and aches, nausea and a fever that breaks and recurs on a number of occasions. Relapsing fever was a new type of typhoid infection. In pre-famine Ireland the population received adequate nourishment from the potato, hence the incidence of relapsing fever was small. The famine conditions resurrected this disease. Cork workhouse hospital and the adjoining fever hospital had inadequate medical personnel and capacity to isolate and quarantine patients. As a result infections not contained, ran rampant throughout the house.

Medical responses to the dysentery and typhoid fever outbreaks were limited. According to Popham, Dover's Powder was the main medicinal application together with 'regular sponging with tepid water, judicious nourishment and above all good nurse tenders'.[63] Inmates received allowances of wine and porter as stimulants to break their fevers. The provision lists in the minutes highlight the increasing reliance on supplies of wine and porter during 1847 to 1849. Physicians encountered difficulty when ordering alcoholic supplies. As physicians they could make allowances for such in the dietary rations but often the guardians alluded to the expense involved. In 1847 the *Cork Examiner* reported that Dr Lyons, a guardian, had stated that the physicians should be viewed in a different light from the other officers of the house. Lyons stated that,

> they could not be denied from requiring to be furnished with whatever they required necessary to the safety of the patients. The idea of preventing them from ordering wine was as if they conceived that their patients needed it was as absurd as hindering them from ordering too much.[64]

Dr O'Connor threatened the guardians that he would report them to the commissioners if they would not resolve it amongst themselves to order wine.[65] Meanwhile whiskey was also administered countrywide for medicinal purposes, being perceived as an economic stimulant by the commissioners. 'Whiskey is fully as good a

stimulant as brandy and its use is therefore recommended as a substitute for the more expensive article and in some cases porter and
port wine to which a small quantity of spirits is added had been
found a nutritive stimulant'.[66]

In addition to the alcoholic remedies, the provision lists show
orders for pearle ashes, saltpetre and arrowroot. Ash is a principal
source of potassium in addition to containing all the minerals
essential to the maintenance of life. The most important are calcium, chloride, iodine, iron, phosphorous, sodium and sulphur. Ash
was sometimes used to make saltpetre, which was used as a food
preservative and also as a diuretic. To accommodate those patients
suffering from diarrhoea and to slow the effects of its escalation,
arrowroot was introduced into the diet. Frequently the Indian meal
was inadequate as a starchy resource and arrowroot became a common source of starch that was more easily digested than other forms
of starch. Preparations of arrowroot could be taken warm or cold
when stiffened like a jelly.[67] Dr Townsend, workhouse physician,
relied on blood-letting as a treatment for fever patients in the course
of the famine. Popham states that 'blood-letting was invariably
called for from the beginning and mercury and chalk were used to
check diarrhoea whilst towards the end of the disease opium was
given when watchfulness and diarrhoea prevailed.'[68]

The health and welfare of the inmates from the commencement of the famine was seriously under threat in such an institution. Mortality from disease reached its peak in 1847 with the
severity of the typhus epidemics. The workhouse hospital and fever
hospital constructed in 1846 played an essential role in the care of
inmates during the famine. In 1848 Cork citizens were concerned
not only about the effects of the famine but that the spectre of
cholera might make a reappearance. The memory of the 1832 outbreak was still fresh in their minds.[69] The *Cork Examiner* heightened speculation as to the arrival of Asiatic Cholera, 'the philo-
sophy of cholera as yet abides much in its mysteriousness, this
alarming monster is approaching us fast, the speculators are warn-
ing of its arrival'.[70]

In 1849 a cholera outbreak occurred. The origins of cholera

were a matter for speculation. Its causative agent lay undiscovered until 1883 when the bacteria *vibrio cholerae* was discovered as its origin. Bacteria contained in stools or urine of cholera victims contaminating a water source is the only means by which a person may be infected. While cholera is not a direct consequence of famine, the emaciated state of the paupers contributed to its destructive effect.

With the workhouse overcrowded and two or three communal urine tubs in a dormitory servicing 3–500 inmates it would be increasingly difficult to contain an outbreak. Patients showed symptoms of diarrhoea, vomiting, thirst and circulatory collapse. The first case of cholera noted by the physicians on 9 April 1849, was described as of 'a very malignant type'. Cholera kills by dehydration and kills rapidly, inmates who contracted the disease died within eight hours of the 'premonitory symptoms' having manifested themselves.[71] The death rate amongst cholera victims was at least 50 per cent, as effective treatment for cholera was elusive. Drs Townsend and Popham speculated on their remedy, hence they ordered additional supplies of whiskey and mustard for the relief of cholera patients in the April to May 1849 provisions lists.[72]

Following the appearance of cholera the doctors speculated that exposure to cold and the low health of inmates increased their vulnerability to contract cholera. They recommended that the increased rations of bread received by patients in the hospital should be adopted across the workhouse especially for those inmates who worked outside. The physicians believed early detection was the key to containing the outbreak. They 'had a night watchman appointed to go through the wards at night and to bring to hospital anyone whom he finds to be affected with the premonitory symptoms of cholera.'[73] The physicians made arrangements to 'visit the hospital three times daily; one visit at eight in the morning and the other at nine at night and in the intervals Mr Gardiner will attend to the cases and send for us when necessary'.[74] During one week, 25 April to 2 May, 173 new cases of cholera were detected, 99 were males and 74 were females. The outbreak in the auxiliary house took place on 18 April, nine days after the outbreak at the main workhouse. During this outbreak the physicians noted the relationship between the health of the inmates and their suscepti-bility to cholera.

On 9 May 1849 the physicians noticed 'some signs of the miti-gation of this fearful disease' as evidenced in the reduced numbers of the cases.[75] Ninety-two new cases were observed in the week of 2 to 9 May attacking more males to females, numbering forty-eight and forty-four respectively:

> We have found that a large number of persons suffering from other maladies, have been seized with this disease especially patients who have been for a long time ailing from dysentery or diarrhoea, these cases possess little constitutional vigour and too frequently sink at once.[76]

The source of the cholera, given that its means of transmission is through contaminated water supplies may be found in the minutes preceding the outbreak in April. In March 1849 the master sug-gested that a pump be provided in connection with the well on the Douglas Road, 'to be worked outside the boundary walls so as to supply water to the inmates of the Timber Buildings at present occupying 1,200 inmates'.[77] Dr O'Connor in his report noted cholera in the auxiliary (timber) buildings was 'of very malignant charac-ter, running its course with great rapidity'.[78]

In the same instance the master reported that 'the holders of the land on the east and west sides of the boundary walls do permit cess pools and urine tanks to be constructed on their ground and keep them clean, in consideration they be allowed to keep the contents' (see figure 14).[79] He believed that the relocation of the cess pools and urine tanks would be an 'effective arrangement on avoiding a nuisance which has hitherto been so much complained of'.[80] Contamination may have originated from this relocation of the cess pools and the new water pump. The construction was per-ceived as a means of avoiding a nuisance but in fact it may have contributed to the emergence of the cholera menace.

Thus with the cholera threat eliminated by June 1849 the in-mates' health received some respite but they still experienced outbreaks of fever and disease in addition to other afflictions.

Fig. No. 14: *Lay-out drawing of the workhouse cess pools illustrating the probable cause of the cholera outbreak*

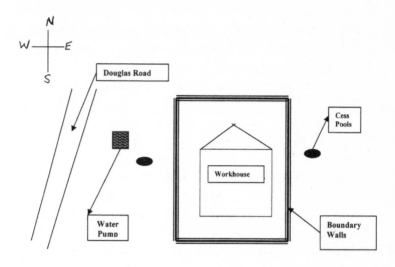

Thus with the cholera threat eliminated by June 1849 the inmates' health received some respite but they still experienced outbreaks of fever and disease in addition to other afflictions.

According to Popham, bronchitis was predominant amongst the aged and infirm category; there 'it rapidly assumed a dynamic character.'[81] Jaundice was common, as was a series of cases showing a resemblance to scarlantia in the 'soreness of the throat and brilliant redness of the tongue'.[82] Instances of smallpox occurred in the 1845 and 1846 but fewer instances of these were noted in the latter years of the famine. The workhouse authorities adopted the resolution of the commissioners to vaccinate persons entering the workhouse against smallpox. Official proceedings for 1845 illustrate that a programme of vaccination against smallpox was initiated in late October 1845 under the 3 and 4 Vic. Cap. 29, Section 6. A letter from the commissioners outlined that the guardians of the union 'shall contract with competent medical practitioners across the union for the period of one year. Thereafter shall enter into renewed contracts on a yearly basis for the vaccination of all persons who may come to them requiring vaccination.'[83] Medical officers were to receive one shilling for the initial 200 successful vaccinations and six pence for subsequent cases. This substantiates the reduction in the recorded number of cases of smallpox in 1846 and 1847 and thereafter it became uncommon. Without the vaccination efforts one can only imagine the increased pressures which the medical staff and inmates would have experienced.

The statistics relating to the workhouse hospital and its adjoining fever hospital illustrate the prevalence of illness and disease during the famine. The numbers of admissions to the hospitals are not definitive regarding the amount of fever cases, since many patients were not removed from the workhouse to the hospital. Hospital accommodation was equally as overcrowded and limited as that of the main workhouse building and in the case of the cholera epidemic many patients died before being removed to an isolated unit. Containing and isolating disease was not a practicable option but rather helped to propagate the pestilence. However, the admissions to the fever hospital and the workhouse infirmary follow the famine's course.

During 1845 the workhouse hospital had a temporary adjoining fever hospital but it did not become a permanent structure until 1846. Patients admitted to the infirmary were either externs or interns, catering also for the lunatics and insane until they were removed to the lunatic asylum during 1846 as referred to earlier.[84] The monthly averages for 1845 can be largely regarded as constants until November when increased admissions to the hospital are evident as a result of the deteriorating health of paupers due to the blight of September. The impact of the famine on the health of inmates becomes more pronounced in 1846 as evinced through the figures in the hospital and the new fever hospital in figure 15. The graph illustrates a two-fold increase in sick patients by 1846. The highest instance occurred in December 1846. Even the new fever house completed after June 1846 afforded little respite from the pressures of famine fever and disease.

The pressure on medical staff was apparent in the minutes, and from February to June 1846 the pages are filled with reports from the buildings committee and Dr O'Connor's recommendations on the site location. In February the guardians resolved to petition parliament 'praying' for the erection of fever hospitals in the rural districts of the union to alleviate pressure on their fever hospital and for these 'to be charged on the rate'.[85] In March 1846 Dr Popham was appointed as an assistant physician to Dr O'Connor to facilitate medical care in the workhouse and the proposed new fever hospital.

Fig. No. 15: Total weekly average per month of patients (including fever hospital, external patients, etc.) at Cork workhouse

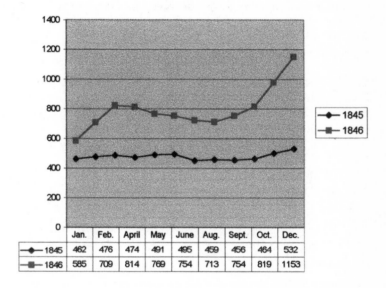

	Jan.	Feb.	April	May	June	Aug.	Sept.	Oct.	Dec.
◆ 1845	462	476	474	491	495	459	456	464	532
■ 1846	585	709	814	769	754	713	754	819	1153

Dr O'Connor, always conscientious about contagion in the air, advised the building committee on the impracticalities of the site, they 'having examined the site are of the opinion that for purposes of ventilation it should be placed in the quarry in preference to the site agreed upon [whereby] it would be 26 feet away from the workhouse and this would remove any infection'.[86] The committee reported that the 'workhouse itself is of a low situation' whilst the fever hospital, if built in the agreed site, then the 'southerly wind accompanied with rain and generally close weather is most adapted to the spread of contagion, which would blow directly onto the whole buildings of the union'.[87] By 30 May plans were underway to relocate to a distance of 340 feet from 'the centre yard of the union workhouse and where the whole of the inmates are congregated during the day', thereby reducing proximity to contagious vapours.[88]

The role of the fever hospital and the workhouse hospital was greatly augmented during 1847. With increased epidemics of fever and other famine illnesses taking hold in the house, the accommodation levels of both hospitals were increased by of temporary wooden buildings. Demand for treatment outstripped availability and from January to June the average monthly total of both hospitals and the temporary sheds was three times that of 1845:

Table No. 23: Average number of patients in the workhouse hospital, fever hospital and the adjoining temporary sheds[89]

Date	1845	1846	1847	1849	1850	1851
Jan.	462	585	1,255	missing	830	1,436
Feb.	476	709	1,801	missing	901	1,571
March	487	825	2,232	965	968	1,681
April	474	814	1,774	900	1,025	1,586
May	491	769	1,461	860	1,023	1,545
June	495	754	1,144	859	966	1,574
July	452	724	missing	898	939	1,408
Aug.	459	713	missing	882	889	1,184
Sept.	456	754	missing	797	799	1,172
Oct.	464	819	missing	839	823	1,201
Nov.	501	982	missing	717	1,123	1,425
Dec.	532	1,153	missing	766	1,247	1,091

The minutes for the latter half of 1847 and 1848 are missing but it is obvious that 1847 was catastrophic. Some semblance of the catastrophe is evident from an account by Father Augustine Maguire who was the chaplain's aid. He recounted his experiences after the famine 'as rapidly as I could give absolution and anointed these poor creatures, they died'.[90] Later he served as a chaplain in the Crimean War and described his experiences there as trivial in comparison 'to watching one's fellow country men dropping dead by the starvation and fever that came on suddenly and gave them no chance to fight'.[91]

Dr Callanan claimed in his report to Popham that 'the obituary of the workhouse for 1847 gives the appalling return of 3,329 deaths, within the month of March 757 inmates perished from famine and fever'.[92]

In 1849, the hospital admissions display a notable increase in March and April, from May onwards there occurred a reduction, thus verifying the physicians' reports that the cholera outbreak of April lasted until June and by July had dissipated. In 1850 increasing patient numbers can be attributed to an overall increase in the capacity of the house to 4,700, after it was reduced in August 1849 from 7,100 to 3,050. Admission trends to the hospitals demonstrate the frequency of disease and fever. They also illustrate the administrative problems of overcrowding and house management, at all times though reflecting the hostile environment in which the inmates resided.

The health and welfare of the inmates was impacted upon by the poor law guidelines. An adherence to dietary regulations, cost effective medicines and perhaps a board of guardians too eager to act, and too humane to comply with warnings on the 'evils' of overcrowding, placed the health of inmates in a precarious predicament. The guardians complained frequently to the commissioners on certain issues but in other issues adhered to their poor law remit. Coping with the vicissitudes of a five-year famine was not the job they had intended to do, their job description was the alleviation of destitution in an institution of strict regulation and regimentation. Inmates, both young and old, were the unfortunate victims of humane responses by officers, be they often incongruous and prejudicial to their health and welfare.

4

THE CHILDREN OF THE HOUSE

Rattle my bones all over the stones,
I'm a poor pauper that nobody owns.

This old Irish famine saying is an adequate reflection of the lack of belonging generally experienced by the many famine victims. It is specifically relevant for the workhouse paupers. Admittance to the workhouse and the prevalence of death, that lurked inside, strengthened this sentiment. Inside the walls of the workhouse the famine took its toll on family members and friends. It enforced a segregation policy amongst men, women and children. Families were divided and feelings of isolation in addition to starvation were everywhere. Many families, although they all resided in the house, were never to see each other again.

Familial separation ensured that families would neither live in the same sections of the workhouse nor communicate with one another. This practice was especially restrictive amongst children entering the workhouse. Children under two years of age were allowed to remain with their mothers. Those aged between two and nine years were accommodated in the nursery wards, while the children aged ten to fifteen years were separated into the boys' ward and the girls' ward. Inevitably these workhouse arrangements, which were devoid of any family conviviality had a psychological impact on the make up and future personalities of these children.

Since the famine conditions became factors in their upbringing, the following questions would consequently arise: how did they perceive themselves? To whom and where did they belong? How would they cope in a 'no family' environment with the absence of parental guidance and example? Parental authority was handed over to the poor law officers under the guise of the workhouse rules. At the kernel of these rules were the guiding principles

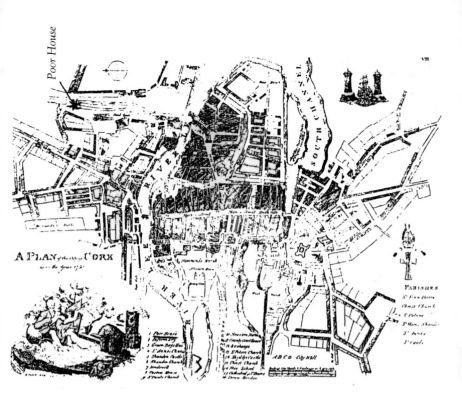

Poor House

Cork poorhouse in 1750, north of the river Lee at the junction of Youghal Road, Lady's Well Street and Sand Quay. A later map [*below*] by Joseph Connor in 1774 puts the poorhouse in the same place

Source: Smith's *History of Cork*, 1750

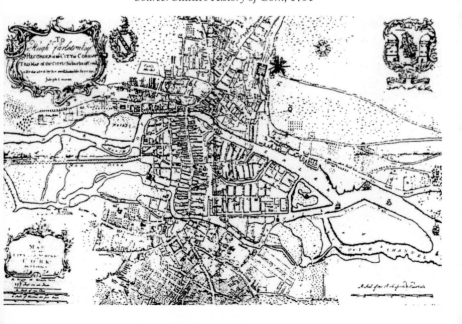

Plan of Cork in 1801 by William Beauford, the poorhouse is near the
Youghal Road as in earlier maps
Source: William O'Sullivan, *Economic History of Cork to 1800*, p. 257

Below right: Cover of a minute book

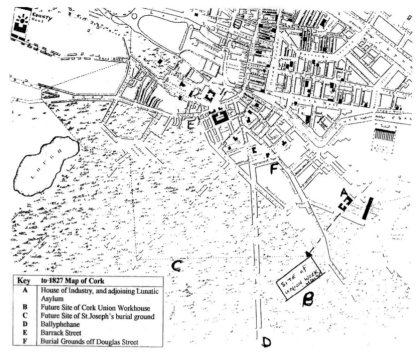

Key	to 1827 Map of Cork
A	House of Industry, and adjoining Lunatic Asylum
B	Future Site of Cork Union Workhouse
C	Future Site of St.Joseph's burial ground
D	Ballyphehane
E	Barrack Street
F	Burial Grounds off Douglas Street

Location of the house of industry in 1827 – south of the river Lee. It performed similar functions to the union workhouse which followed in 1840. The map has been adapted to include a key to the area.

THE USE OF
Indian Meal as an article of Food.

Various Manners of using Indian Meal, as Human Food.

Suppawn, or Porridge, that is to say, boiling milk, or water, thickened with Indian Corn meal. Put into water, this is a breakfast, supper, or dinner for little children; put into milk, it is the same for grown people. In milk it is a good strong meal, sufficient for a man to work upon.

It takes about three pounds and a half of Indian Corn flour to make porridge for ten persons, less than half a pound of corn flour for a meal for one man, and a warm comfortable meal that fills and strengthens the stomach. Three pounds and a half of wheaten flour would make four pounds and a half of bread, but it would be dry bread, and bread alone; and not affording half the sustenance or comfort of the porridge.

Mush.—Put some water or milk into a pot and bring it to boil, then let the corn meal out of one hand gently into the milk or water, and keep stirring with the other, until you have got it into a pretty stiff state; after which let it stand ten minutes or a quarter of an hour, or less, or even only one minute, and then take it out and put it into a dish or bowl. This sort of half pudding half porridge you eat either hot or cold, with a little salt or without it. It is eaten without any liquid matter, but the general way is to have a basin of milk, and taking a lump of the mush you put it into the milk and eat the two together. Here is an excellent pudding, whether eaten with milk or without it; and where there is no milk, it is an excellent substitute for bread, whether you take it hot or cold. It is neither hard or lumpy when cold, but quite light and digestible for the most feeble stomachs. The Indian Corn flour is more wholesome than wheat flour in all its manners of cooking. It is a great convenience for the workman in the field that mush can be eaten cold. It is, in fact, moist bread, and habit soon makes it pleasanter than bread. It is a great thing for all classes of persons, but particularly for the labourer. He may have bread every day, and he may have it hot or cold, and there is more nutrition in it than you can get out of the same quantity of wheat flour. It is eaten at the best tables in America almost every day; some like it hot, some cold, some with milk, some to slice it down and eat it with meat; some like it best made with water, others with milk, but all like it in one way or another. Some put these cold slices again into the oven and eat them hot, or they might be heated on the griddle. It is believed in America that the Indian Corn, even used in this one single manner, does more, as food for man, than all the wheat that is grown in the country, though the flour from that wheat is acknowledged to be the best in the world.

The usual mode of making bread or cake of Indian meal, is to scald the meal in boiling water, and make it of a proper consistency of dough, and bake it on tins before the fire or on griddles half an inch thick; and at the South and West, it is made three quarters of an inch thick. It is Indian Meal, water, and salt, of a consistency to roll out on a tin board, or flatten out with the hands.

It is also made into gruel, or thicker into hasty pudding, by stirring the meal into hot water gradually until it is of a consistency of starch, or a very soft pudding, which hardens as it becomes cold.

It is eaten with butter, fat, salt, or sugar, or treacle, or any relish of salt meat or fish, OR ALONE.

It also makes an excellent cake, by mixing it with coarse flour, in the proportions of two-thirds of Indian meal, and one-third flour.

No mistake can be made in using the meal, as it *can be mixed with, or adapted to anything.*

To Make Excellent Bread without Yeast.—Scald about two handfuls of Indian meal, into which put a little salt, and as much cold water as will make it rather warmer than new milk; then stir in wheat flour, or oatmeal, till it is as thick as a family pudding, and set it down by the fire to rise. In about half an hour it generally grows thin; you may sprinkle a little fresh flour on the top, and mind to turn the pot round, that it may not bake to the side of it. In three or four hours, if you mind the above directions, it will rise and ferment as if you had set it with hop yeast; when it does, make it up in soft dough, flour a pan, put in your bread, set it before the fire, covered up, turn it round to make it equally warm, and in about half an hour it will be light enough to bake.

Hasty Pudding.—Boil water, a quart, three pints, or two quarts according to the size of your family; sift your meal, stir five or six spoonfuls of it thoroughly into a bowl of water; when the water in the kettle boils, pour into it the contents of the bowl; stir it well and let it boil up thick; put in salt to suit your own taste, then stand over the kettle and sprinkle in meal, handful after handful, stirring it very thoroughly all the time, and letting it boil between whiles. When it is so thick that you stir it with difficulty, it is about right. It takes about half an hour's cooking. Eat it with milk or treacle, or alone.

☞ *Be careful to observe, that Indian Corn in all its preparations requires to be well boiled or baked.*

GEORGE PURCELL & CO., Machine Printers, Cork.

Source for 'Indian meal' is a pamphlet in the Cork Archives

13th *December*, 1845.

SIR,

HAVING received a communication from the Poor Law Commissioners, dated the 6th instant, relative to the disease amongst Potatoes, and matter connected therewith, I beg to forward to you the following extract from the Circular of the Commissioners :—

" THE Poor Law Commissioners are desirous of obtaining from time to time, for the Com- " missioners appointed by His Excellency the Lord Lieutenant in reference to the apprehended " Scarcity, information respecting the extent and progress of disease amongst Potatoes, and respect- " ing other matters of interest which may have connexion, either directly or indirectly, with such " disease.

" They propose to place themselves in communication with the Boards of Guardians through- " out Ireland, for this purpose. It appears to them, that if each individual Guardian would impart " to the Board of which he is a Member, at its weekly Meeting, the results of his experience and " observation in his own locality, and the Board of Guardians, through its Clerk, would correspond " with the Poor Law Commissioners on this subject, a valuable body of information might be col- " lected, which would have a tendency to prevent either supineness or exaggerated alarm.

" With this view, the Poor Law Commissioners transmit herewith to you, Copies of a " Circular of Questions : and they have to request that you will forward a Copy to each of the Guar- " dians of your Union ; conveying to each at the same time, the request of the Poor Law Commis- " sioners, that he will kindly undertake to read the Questions attentively, and to contribute according " to the measure of his knowledge, to their being correctly answered by the Board of Guardians " collectively, when they shall be finally submitted to such Board for consideration."

I accordingly enclose herewith a copy of the Queries referred to in the Commissioners' Circular; conveying to you at the same time their request, that you will be good enough to give your attention to the subject, and to favour the Board with the result of your experience on the questions adverted to, to the end that the inquiries may be correctly answered by the Board of Guardians collectively, when submitted to them for consideration.

I beg to add, that the Letter of the Commissioners and the Queries inclosed therewith, will be brought under the consideration of the Board of Guardians in the first instance at their next Meeting, on the 15th instant, and subsequently at their future Meetings from time to time, as occasion may render necessary.

I have the honour to be,

SIR,

Your very obedient Servant,

Clerk of the Guardians.

To

Guardian of *Union.*

Letter to Richard Dowden, 1845, outlining response from the poor law commissioners' circular on the 'scarcity of potatoes'

TO THE COMMITTEE OF THE CORK DISPENSARY AND HUMANE SOCIETY.

GENTLEMEN,

Since our last Annual Report, your City has been comparatively free from any epidemic disease, the numbers relieved within the past year amounting to 9,661, while those of the preceding reached to 26,043.

When alluding in our last to the great extent of the late epidemics, we observed "that this vast amount of disease had been caused chiefly by Fever, as also by Dysentry and Influenza," neither of which we are happy to say have prevailed to any alarming extent for some months. On that occasion we called particular attention to the filthy state of Cork; we beg again to remark that a sanitary condition of your City would tend powerfully to check any future epidemic, by acting on the principle of an old and true saying, viz., "Prevention is better than cure." This under present apprehensions forcibly applies to the Cholera, whose outbreak amongst us is only a matter of time; we therefore trust, that the recent nuisance act will be carried into prompt and immediate effect.

We cannot allow the present opportunity to pass without calling attention to our letter of the 13th October, 1847, addressed to your Committee, wherein we urge the necessity of changing the locality of the Dispensary, and beg to impress for the reasons so fully stated, the propriety of your entertaining as speedily as circumstances will allow, the subject matter referred to in that document.

We have the honor to remain

Your's obedient Servants,

RICHARD T. FOWLER, M. D. Chairman.
JOHN W. FLYNN, M. D.
P. J. BARRY, M. D.
THOS. GREGG, M. D.
JOSEPH HARRISON, M. D.
CHS. ARMSTRONG, M. D.
JOHN MURPHY, M. D.
THOS. WALL, M. D. Resident Surgeon.

ABSTRACT OF CASH ACCOUNT.

Received.		Paid.	
Balance of last year, ... £ 15 15 4		For Drugs, Calico, Paper for Blisters, Warm Plasters, &c.... .... £112 5 9	
180 Subscriptions, amounting to.. .... 220 15 6		Salaries of Physicians, Apothecary, Porter, Bleeder, and Collector of Subscriptions, ... 310 14 0	
8 Donations, ... 14 7 0		Rent, 1 year to March 25th 1847,.. .... 23 0 0	
2 Presentments,.... .... 272 9 6		Spirits, Wine, Vinegar, &c.. .... 24 13 8	
		Lard, Oil, Turpentine, Sugar, Molasses, &c. .. 34 18 2	
		Rewards in Drowning Cases, ... 10 0	
		Incidental Charges, as Coals, Stationery, Printing, &c.,.. .... 17 5 9	
£523 7 4		£523 7 4	

⁎ *Balances due Physicians, Apothecary, Druggist, 2 Years Rent, Paper, Vinegar, Turpentine, Spirits, &c., &c., £346 12 9.*

PRESIDENTS.

BISHOP OF CORK,	THE MAYOR OF CORK,	DAN MURPHY,
RT. REV. DR. DELANEY,	THE DEAN OF CORK,	MAJOR N. L. BEAMISH.

GENERAL COMMITTEE.

JOHN BALLARD,	W. HARVEY,	JAMES HOGG,	WM. CLEAR,
N. CUMMINS,	J. J. GALLWEY,	J. DUNBAR,	ABM. ABELL, M.R.I.A.
D. DONEGAN,	TIMOTHY MAHONY,	CAPT. WESTROPP,	J. W. TOPP.
W. SHERLOCK,	DAN MEAGHER,	JOHN COTTER,	

PHYSICIANS.

DR. FOWLER,	DR. BARRY,	DR. HARRISON,	DR. MURPHY,
DR. O'FLYNN,	DR. GREGG,	DR. ARMSTRONG,	

SURGEON AND APOTHECARY,.......... **THOMAS WALL, M. D.**

Extract from the Cork Dispensary and Humane Society
Source: Cork Archives

Debit Maintenance Account,
Credit Provision Account, } - - - 507. 11. 3¾

And the average cost of a Pauper for the week was — 2 „ 3.

The Master's estimate of Provisions and Necessaries required for the ensuing week was examined, and Orders were duly made for the several articles specified, namely :

33.000 lbs Bread
3 Tons Indian Meal
3 Tons Oatmeal
3707 Gallons Milk
8 Cwt Salt
1 Chest Tea
672 lbs Sugar
70 lbs arrow Root
100 lbs Rice
30 lts Pepper

2 dozen Wine
3 Barrels Porter
93 ¾ Fowls
23 lts Butter
295 Gallons New milk
200 lts Candles

The following Books were also produced by the Clerk, their accuracy having been previously ascertained by him, and authenticated by his Signature :

1. The several Clothing Accounts.
2. The Medical Officers' Books.

On the Report and recommendation of the Finance Committee, the following Bills having been duly examined, and found to be correct, and in accordance with the several Orders, were directed to be paid, and Cheques for the several amounts were duly drawn on the Treasurer, and Signed, namely :

Sample provision list from minute book of Cork union

P

William Crawford Esquire was unanimously Elected Chairman

and

Samuel Lane Esquire and Joseph Hayes Esquire Vice Chairman and Deputy Vice Chairman for the Year ensuing

The following Bye Laws were Submitted to the meeting Seriatim and unanimously adopted

Resolved. That to insure regularity and order in the proceedings of this Board, The following Bye Laws be adopted

First. That every Guardian when he desires to speak, shall stand up and address the Chairman, and at all other times observe strict Silence, and attend to the Matter under discussion; and if two or more Guardians rise to speak at the same time the Chairman shall decide to whom the priority of speaking belongs, and upon his naming the individual, the other Guardian shall resume their Seats

Secondly, That all Motions (Except for the admission or rejection of applicants) shall be submitted to the Board in Writing by the Mover, and if seconded, shall be discussed and unless withdrawn by the Mover and Seconder; shall be determined by open Vote

Thirdly, That no Guardian except the mover shall speak more than once

Extract of resolutions adopted by Cork board of guardians at first meeting of discipline, order and a constant element of subjugation. Subjugation to the workhouse rules amounted to an affirmation by all inmates, child and adult, that they were by the 'test of destitution' lower than the lowest pauper outside the workhouse relief system.

Children are impressionable innocents and one can only estimate the nature of the long-term impact of the workhouse regime on them. Commentators on the condition of workhouse children always echo the opinion that these children were old before their time and were denied their childhood innocence. The workhouses did not only receive children accompanied by their parents and families. The indoor registers for Cork union workhouse show large numbers of orphans, deserted children and foundlings. These children when registered were often described in an inferior manner. These entries refer to their status at birth or their general appearance and health. They often hint that these innocents were responsible both for their circumstances of birth whether they be 'illegitimate, bastard or pauper'. Therefore 'innocents' is an appropriate description for all child victims of the workhouse administration during the famine years.

The indoor registers are the principal source of data regarding the pauper children. The directive of the 1 and 2 Victoria Cap. 56, Section 42, required that all inmates be classified upon registration under fourteen categories. The categories most relevant to the admission of children were: name and surname of pauper, age, sex, religious denomination, whether orphan, deserted, bastard or admitted with family. If disabled, a description of disability, observations on the condition of the pauper when admitted, the electoral division or townland in which resident, date of admission, date of birth and whether legitimate or illegitimate and the date of discharge from or death within the workhouse.

Children under the age of sixteen constituted between 33 and 40 per cent of the pauper host in England during the mid-nineteenth century.[1] This statistic was borne out in the case of the Irish workhouses in the years preceding the 'hungry 1840s'. However during the famine, this figure escalated. Calculations of inmate figures for the Cork union workhouse illustrate an increase on the

English situation. Between 1845 and 1851, 50 to 60 per cent of the inmate population comprised children aged fifteen and under.

The months preceding the blight highlight Felix Driver's observation. In Cork workhouse from January to September 1845 this figure varied from 34 to 37 per cent. The autumn of 1846 witnessed a second potato failure accompanied by an increased threat of starvation and death. Hence admissions rose, largely whole families made totally destitute by an over reliance on a single food source. As a consequence, the number of children in the workhouse grew from 37 to 43 per cent by November of 1846. During the worst year Black '47 it escalated to 60 per cent in January, but then levelled off to a figure that fluctuated between 42 and 59 per cent in the period February 1847 to July 1851.

Table No. 24: Percentage of workhouse inmates aged 15 years and under[2]

Date	1845	1846	1847	1849	1850	1851
Jan.	34	33	60		44	49
Feb.	34	37	42		49	52
Mar.	35	38	40	45	48	51
Apr.	35	38	32	45	49	52
May	36	39	40	45	50	50
June	37	38	43	45	51	51
July	36	39		46	51	54
Aug.	37	39		50	57	63
Sept.	38	42		54	59	63
Oct.	37	42		52	58	60
Nov.	38	43		51	56	58
Dec.	39	42		54	54	57

To explain such a vast increase in the child population of the Cork workhouse, it is necessary to look at factors other than the simple explanation of famine. These factors are linked to the data to be found in the minutes and registers regarding the 'child class of paupers' with reference to their parentage, physical condition, education and figures regarding admission, mortality, births and illegitimacy.

Workhouse commentators argue that assessing children on

the criteria outlined in the indoor registers was cruel and unfair, especially those entries that required details of birth. They maintain the poor law officers' pre-supposed children to be agents of their own pauperism, deliberately selecting to be born into the pauper class. Instead they were the innocent victims of the circumstances of their birth. One such commentator puts it, 'Children do not catch pauperism as they catch measles'.[3]

This quote highlights that the poor law administrators were unyielding on the principle of separating the family unit. Under the workhouse admission regulations children were separated according to age and gender. The authorities maintained that an enforced separation of children from the adult paupers would reduce the likelihood of them becoming paupers in adult life. The poor law theoreticians perceived pauperism as contagious and aspired to control it through a policy of non-communication between adult and young inmates and making it compulsory for children to attend the workhouse school. It was envisaged that children would be less inclined to choose an idle lifestyle, and perhaps leave the workhouse with a skill or trade.

In reality the mentality of the poor law theoreticians was grounded less on the philanthropic principle of educating pauper children but more on the semiotics of deterrence. It was hoped that by making conditions as uninviting as possible that it would act as a deterrent to admission. For existing inmates it would increase their motivation for early discharge as they longed to return to their family units once again. This would have the two-fold effect of reducing dependency upon the poor law and consequently reduce union expenditure. Circumstances changed in 1845. The poor law administrators encountered the effects of climatic conditions upon the staple diet of an entire country. Faced with a crisis, the policy of making the workhouse appear as uninviting as possible failed. Consequently, admissions of both adults and children to the workhouse increased. The natural impulse of survival together with the natural instinct of parents that their children survive occasioned a rise in child admissions.

The minute books record the admission of children in three

categories.[4] In 1845 the total number of admissions of males under fifteen years was 649, females under fifteen years numbered 571 and 401 infants under two years.

Table No. 25: Yearly admission figures of children under fifteen years to Cork workhouse[5]

Yearly Admissions	1845	1846	1847	1849	1850	1851
Males under 15 years	649	2,176	1,516	2,616	3,102	combined
Females under 15 years	571	1,891	1,253	2,377	2,608	5,162
Children under 2 years	401	1,382	568	671	858	777
Total Child Admissions	**1,612**	**5,449**	**3,337**	**5,664**	**6,568**	**5,939**

The first notable effect of the potato failure upon the children of Cork union was witnessed in November 1845. Admissions rose across all three age categories. In the cases of the males and females under fifteen, it increased by 50 per cent in October, while the number of admissions of children under the age of two doubled from nineteen in October to thirty-seven in November. Children formed between 37 and 38 per cent of the entire workhouse population in these months. Despite this increase the figure was still within the expected levels as exemplified by the English workhouses, i.e. 33 to 40 per cent. Since the poor law was designed to cater for a greater pauper class in Ireland, the house was able to accommodate this small but telling increase in 1845.

Judging by the admission trend of children during January to September 1845 it was apparent that a change was occurring. An external element was forcing more families and children into the workhouse for reasons other than financial destitution. The imminent prospect of starvation accompanied with the possibility of death was felt across the pauper class of the union. As their main source of nourishment, the potato, was eliminated from their diet, the workhouse became their last resort irrespective of the reputation that surrounded the workhouse. There, at least they would receive rations however meagre and the children would be clothed and sheltered. Separation was the price the family unit paid for its chance at survival. In numerous instances the Cork minute books record cases of women and children pleading destitution due to their husband's desertion to feign entry, only later to be prosecuted because these were not *bona fide* desertion cases. These were the trends emerging at the close of 1845, which escalated intensely in the following years 1846–50.

With the dawning of 1846 came an unprecedented rise in child admissions. In January the figures doubled, 119 boys under fifteen years were admitted, 102 girls under fifteen years and 83 infants under two. Overall child admissions for the year amounted to 5,449, almost treble the capacity of the entire workhouse. However, children did not remain in the workhouse for the duration of the year. The trends within the three categories; boys, girls and infants under the age of two, escalated also, though at all times the admission numbers of boys were greater than those of girls. The number of infants was less than the females. This pattern was reflected annually. In 1846, 2,176 boys, 1,891 girls and 1,382 infants sought refuge in Cork workhouse.

From January to June 1846, the impact of the increased rate of admissions was obvious across the child categories. The guardians noticed a sharp rise in the numbers soliciting admittance. Necessity dictated the guardians notify the poor law commissioners in Dublin on 23 February. The influx of paupers was 'so great and their admission on account of their utter destitution so imperative that on this day, this house contains 2,480 paupers being 480 more than it was meant to accommodate'.[6] The letter received from the commissioners did not adequately address the problem. It extolled the necessity of maintaining the workhouse capacity and cautioned the guardians that 'excessive crowding of inmates is an evil to be guarded against and the commissioners earnestly desire the especial attention of the guardians to this point'.[7]

'Excessive crowding' was not avoided in the year 1846; admissions of children amounted to 5,449. These were proportioned as follows: 25 per cent infants under two years, 41 per cent males under fifteen years and 34 per cent females under fifteen years.

From June to August 1846 there was a seasonal decline; admissions tended to be fewer in the summer months. Numbers of child admissions exploded in late August, peaking in October and November. In November 365 boys, 327 girls and 174 infants were admitted, almost half the capacity of the workhouse which was still unchanged at 2,000. Table 26 traces the child and adolescent admissions for the year 1846.

Table No. 26: Child and adolescent admissions for selected months in 1846

1846	Jan.	Feb.	Mar.	May	June	July	Aug.	Sept.	Nov.	Dec.
Males under 15 years	119	137	125	136	88	87	149	144	365	253
Females under 15 years	102	111	105	109	81	79	125	123	327	284
Children under 2 years	83	85	65	93	82	88	144	123	174	143

As with the trends of 1845 and 1846, the patterns of a greater number of boys to girls seeking admissions, and a greater number of girls in comparison to the number of infant admissions were evident once more. In 1846, there occurred a two-fold increase in admissions across all three categories of child and adolescent admissions. In the period January to June 1846, admissions of females aged two to fifteen years numbered 1,891. In the corresponding period in 1847, there were 1,253 admissions to the same category as visible from the tables below and over. In total 3,337 children under the age of fifteen years gained entry. Infants under two years comprised 17 per cent, girls aged two to fifteen years 38 per cent and boys aged two to fifteen years 45 per cent.

Table No. 27: Comparison of admission figures for children under 15 years, Jan. to June 1846 & 1847

	Males under 15 years	Females under 15 years	Children under 2 years
Jan.–June 1846	2,176	1,891	1,382
Jan.–June 1847	1,516	1,253	568

Table No. 28: Child admissions for January to June 1847

1847	Jan.	Feb.	Mar.	April	May	June
Males (2–15 years)	721	286	243	18	205	43
Females (2–15 years)	573	207	240	20	175	38
Children under 2	310	102	91	1	52	12

Meanwhile the percentage composition of all workhouse inmates that were aged fifteen and under remained relatively constant give or take a five per cent variable increase. There was one exception that of January 1847 when the percentage composition of children reached 60 per cent. It was not to reach a similar recorded level until 1851.

In August 1851, 63 per cent of inmates were children. This is explained by the fact that the capacity of the house then was 6,200.[8] The worst excesses of the famine had dissipated by 1851 and the workhouse consisted of more long-term admissions of children. Sampling from the indoor registers for this period produces evidence of an increased number of orphans. Between 67 and 70 per cent of child admissions were categorised as orphans:

Table No. 29.1: No-parent children admitted Mar. 1840–Aug. 1842, categorised as orphan & deserted

Deserted Children	Orphaned Children
47%	53%

Table No. 29.2: No-parent children admitted Mar. 1848–Aug. 1850, categorised as orphan & deserted & foundling

Deserted Children	Orphaned Children	Foundlings
31%	67%	2%

In 1847 the numbers in receipt of workhouse relief were frequently double the capacity of the house which was 2,800. The reasoning for this large proportion of 60 per cent of child inmates in January 1847 was founded on the continuing severe winter 'season of scarcity' and the rampant typhus fever of 1846 which especially affected children. Parents responded by lodging their children, albeit temporarily, in the workhouse. Recorded proceedings for 1846 and the initial six months of 1847 display large numbers of 'deserted women and children'. Often women and children pleaded destitution on the grounds of desertion by their husbands. The reality was either of two situations; the men hoped to earn money to buy alternate foodstuffs by working in a public works scheme or else they had emigrated. In both cases residency periods for children tended to be relatively short, usually until the false nature of their 'desertion' was uncovered or until their parents were discharged. This explains the increased volume of children in the workhouse in January 1847.

1847 established itself in memory, as one of the worst years of the famine but 1849 was equally poignant in terms of its impact within Cork workhouse. The impact is most noticeable in cases of deserted or orphaned children. Statistical analysis for 1849 is calculated from returns for ten months, March to December. The minute book (BG 69 A8) for the previous months is missing. The trends in the age categories are again consistent with the earlier years. In the course of the ten months, 2,616 boys and 2,377 girls between the ages of two and fifteen and 671 infants under two years were admitted. The capacity of the workhouse was increased to accommodate between 6,300 and 7,100 inmates during the period March to September 1849. Increased house capacity allowed for additional admissions across all inmate categories. Thereafter it was reduced to between 3,050 and 4,700 in accordance with the subsequent reduction in admission numbers.

Contrasting 1849 to 1846 it is clear that despite the high mortality and the proliferation of disease in 1849, the actual total number of child admissions did not double as in 1846 and 1847 but came within the parameters of the house capacity which fluctuated between 4,700 and 7,100. This illustrates that although the admissions increased, the spatial impact was somewhat reduced thereby providing somewhat less congested conditions.

In 1849 the percentage of all workhouse inmates under fifteen years increased from 3 to 11 per cent on the figure for 1847. In March 45 per cent, August 50 per cent and by December 54 per cent of all workhouse inmates were children. This increase was attributable to a diversity of factors. Firstly, increased cases of both children and of mothers with their children. Secondly, the impact of augmented mortality across all age groups. Mortality figures for women above the age of fifteen in the years 1845 to 1850 were inclined to be slightly higher than the figures of men in the same age grouping. An assumption can be made that a number of children lost their mothers while residing in the workhouse thereby increasing the percentage of children who became long-term inmates of the workhouse. Thirdly, increased numbers of foundlings and orphans were admitted, again contributing to the number of 'long-term' residents.

Table 29 illustrates the demographic factors in relation to the 'class' of children admitted to the workhouse, in terms of child desertion, orphaned or foundlings. In the period March 1848 to August 1850, the numbers of children admitted into the workhouse without a parent were as follows: 67 per cent were orphaned, almost twice that of deserted children (with no parent) at 31 per cent and 2 per cent were foundlings.[9]

Of fifty admissions (both adult and child) for the week 3 March to 10 March 1849, thirty-two were children under the age of fifteen. The thirty-two children consisted of thirteen orphans and eight deserted children. Of the recorded child admissions (with no parent) in a particular week 62 per cent were orphans and 38 per cent were deserted.[10] There was a consistency in the period March 1848 to August 1850. It further reveals that 68 per cent of recorded admissions of children were either deserted or orphaned and only 20 per cent of child admissions were accompanied by a parent or relative.

An investigation of the same 'classes' of children prior to the famine (in the same period March 1840 to August 1842) shows that 53 per cent of children were orphaned and 47 per cent of children were deserted. By August 1850 the percentage of orphaned children had increased to 68 per cent again emphasising the impact of the famine. It alludes to the lack of belonging experienced by the workhouse innocents. For many the old Irish saying was especially true 'I'm a poor pauper that nobody owns'. Children admitted to the house in 1849 suffered the worst in many respects. Statistical evidence reveals the famine experience for child inmates and their increased susceptibility to disease especially during the cholera epidemic of the late spring and summer of 1849.

In the indoor register for the years 1850 and 1851 the impact of the famine is evident through detailed accounts of orphaned and deserted children. Their parents were either dead, imprisoned for stealing or in the case of single-parent families the father had emigrated. The Haly brothers, from 'Glownthawn', Daniel aged twelve, William aged ten and Tim aged seven, were all admitted to the workhouse in June 1850 for one month. Their father was dead and their mother was in the gaol. Their case was not uncommon. The proportion of children in the workhouse peaked in July and August 1851 at 63 per cent.

This peak was attributed to the intrusion of the famine upon the family unit. Numerous examples of foundlings and deserted children 'with no family or friends' are entered in the indoor register for the period. Descriptions of orphans and foundlings wearing union clothing at admission suggested children were repeatedly admitted. William Holland, aged fourteen years, was found as an orphan in July 1851 wearing union clothing. Due to his age it is probable that he was an inmate of the house at the height of the famine. This was possibly the case with Ellen Callaghan born in 1835. The indoor register for the period 1841 records a girl aged five from Carrignavar admitted with her mother.[11] Recorded in 1848 is an Ellen Callaghan now aged fourteen, with her three sisters Margaret aged twelve, Mary aged seven and Hanora aged two. All were from Carrignavar. All were described as having 'no friends or family'.[12] It is highly probable that the Callaghan girls experienced the horrors of the famine, with the likely deaths of their parents occurring in 1849–51, as the youngest was only two years old upon admission.

These individual cases reveal that children entering the workhouse in 1850–51 were burdened with personal horrors of morbidity and disease. Many were still convalescent after the severe cholera and dysentery epidemics of 1849. Such was the scenario with Hanora Mullane, an orphan aged fourteen, who came to the Cork workhouse from the Barrack Street fever hospital in July 1850 for convalescence.

The admission figures for 1845 to 1851 indicate the role which the workhouse would adopt in the case of children. Rather than solely being correctional or penological, the role synthesised shelter, education and guidance in lieu of parental support. The Cork board of guardians was not a foundling institution but a poor law institution. It adhered to the penal nature of the poor law regulations. It did not legislate for compassionate treatment of children but responded to their most basic requirements. Therefore the institutional culture of the house impacted upon the young inmates. A commentator who visited Cork workhouse after the famine in 1852 provided the following account:

> Never did I visit any dungeon, any abode of crime or misery, in any country, which left the same crushing sense of sorrow, indignation and compassion – almost despair … charity is as much charity in the Christian sense as the praying machines of the Tartars is piety.[13]

Under the workhouse regime it was inevitable that childhood innocence waned only to be replaced with a gripping mortality and proliferation of disease. Following the publication of John Arnott's investigation into the condition of children in the Cork workhouse it was branded a 'chamber of horrors' in the *Daily Express*.

A 'chamber of horrors' is a lucid description for the high mortality rates and the increased vulnerability amongst the workhouse children to disease and contagion.[14] Examination of the mortality figures discloses the undeniably cruel impact of the famine as it terminated both the lives and families of children. As with previous evidence, the mortality figures are derived from the returns in the minute books.[15] Analysis is therefore based on all recorded data and occasionally suppositions must be made to examine the evidence further.

From 1845 to 1850, the minute books record 3,267 cases of

child mortality. The number of recorded deaths in each category is as follows: 1,084 males between the ages of two and fifteen years, 991 females between the ages two and fifteen years and 1,192 infants under two years.

Table No. 30: Yearly mortality figures

Yearly Mortality	1845	1846	1847	1849	1850	1851
Males under 15	56	91	485	290	162	Combined
Females under 15	52	48	487	195	209	474
Children under 2	108	245	409	216	214	312
Total	216	384	1,381	701	585	726

In a corresponding post-famine period from 1852 to 1857, John Arnott puts the number of child deaths at 2,149.[16] This was approximately 1,000 less than the figure calculated from official proceedings during the famine. There was an obvious decline in the post famine period. However this decline was much steeper than a reduction of 1,000 deaths, given that almost two years of the famine records are missing. Figures in the minute books portray 1847 as the most calamitous of the famine years, therefore one can assume that the latter half of 1847 was the same if not worse than the first.

1848 saw a slight downturn in figures and by inserting the average number of deaths per month for the first two months of 1849 the following estimates may be derived. The estimated total of child deaths in the period 1845 to 1850 was 7,825 categorised as follows:

Males aged two to fifteen years	2,659
Females aged two to fifteen years	2,439
Infants aged under two years	2,727

Using the estimations as a guideline, the decline in the number of child deaths from 1852 to 1857 is approximately 3–4,000. This figure can be explained by the fact that the capacity of the workhouse increased in the post famine years, hence more admissions could be accommodated and death figures would have risen accordingly. Arnott claims in his investigation in 1859 that the mortality was quite high then due to the inferior housing conditions and the poor workhouse diet which provoked death. If this was the child's experience in 1859, then the immediate impact of the famine was evidently more appalling and morose for the children of the house.

Two hundred and sixteen child deaths for the year 1845, when examined shows a marginally higher number of male deaths, with fifty-six male deaths recorded in comparison to fifty-two female deaths (under fifteen years). The infant category (boys and girls under two years of age) was more susceptible. In 1845 there occurred 108 infant deaths, equalling the combined total of boys and girls who died in the age category two to fifteen years. In 1846 these patterns are replicated. The male figure of ninety-one deaths was almost double the female number of forty-eight deaths. Figures show that although male mortality was higher in the overall numbers, in fact there was little deviation between both categories. The only area of deviation occurred in January to March when female death figures increased and male deaths receded.

Numbers for infant deaths continued to escalate in 1846 to 245 deaths. This figure was double the previous year's figure. Famine conditions were not experienced for the entire year in 1845, the blight initially appeared in September 1845 and it was a few months before its effects were evident. Therefore 1845 mortality figures can be considered largely as the norm.

From the death figures of 1846, it was apparent that those children in the infant category had the least chance of survival. 1846 witnessed an increase in diseases, especially in relapsing and remittent fever, both of which germinated from the unsanitary conditions in the overcrowded workhouse. The workhouse physician Dr O'Connor explained to the master, his observations of the 'unusual number of fever cases' among the infants where 'the number of fever cases returned as sixty, in explanation from the Professor, forty of these cases were infants, and all were cases of high fever'.[17] Infant vulnerability to the fever explains the increased incidence of death in this category, which is evident from table 31:

Table No. 31: Child mortality for selected months in 1846

1846	Jan	Mar	Apr	June	July	Sept	Oct	Dec
Male mortality under 15 years	7	4	9	0	0	0	4	39
Female mortality under 15 years	2	6	4	1	1	2	2	42
Child mortality under 2 years	17	14	23	8	4	12	18	60

Child admissions numbered 5,449 in 1846. Despite an increase in admissions the actual number of child deaths as a percentage of child admissions was 7 per cent. The figure for the previous year (in the same period) was 14 per cent. Given that the famine conditions were chronically worse in 1846 than at the end of 1845, the percentage of child deaths to admissions appears low. In explanation admissions in 1846 were greater than 1845, capacity remained the same and hence admissions tended to be short in duration. For many inmates their terms of residency amounted to a few days up to a few weeks in duration. With a constant tide of children into the workhouse many were admitted for a short period to receive some relief rations rather than nothing at all. At one point in 1846 the guardians took upon themselves 'the privilege of giving admission tickets to any destitute poor person, to be admitted provisionally until examined before the board'.[18] The policy of provisional admission would thus swell overall admissions and consequently the numbers of the child deaths to child admissions would surely vary from the 1845 figures.

In a six-month period January to June 1847, 1,381 child deaths were recorded amounting to 42 per cent of all child admissions for that period. All categories of child admissions experienced an increase during January to March. The infant category was the first to indicate that the worst excesses of the 1846 winter and the New Year were over. A 50 per cent reduction in the number of infant deaths occurred from February to March 1847, from 122 to 67 respectively. A month later the male and female categories declined accordingly. By June the number had reduced dramatically but it was still higher than the previous June.

Table No. 32: Child and adolescent monthly mortality, Jan–June 1847

1847	Jan	Feb	Mar	Apr	May	June
Male mortality (2 to 15 years)	55	111	120	88	73	38
Female mortality (2 to 15 years)	41	112	139	100	66	29
Child mortality under 2 years	81	122	67	79	39	21

Table 31 shows no male death, one female and eight infant deaths for June 1846. The result of the dramatic reduction in the infant category from February to March balances out the child deaths almost equally between the three categories. In 1847, 1,381 deaths were divided as follows, 35 per cent males, 35 per cent females between two and fifteen years and 30 per cent children less than two years. A growth in the numbers of recorded deaths is seen across all sectors of children for January to June 1847. The figure for that six-month period is quadruple the number for 1846. This higher number in 1847 is attributable to increased admissions, small sporadic increases in workhouse capacity, continued fever outbreaks and general contagion. If all the evidence were available it would not be an exaggeration to expect child mortality figures to total approximately 2,700 in 1847.

The 1849 mortality figure is significantly lower than 1847. It is still however higher than 1846. During ten months there were 5,664 child admissions of which 12 per cent, 701, died. In table 33 the admission figures for 1849 (although for ten months) are similar to those of 1846. The capacity of the house had increased by 4,000 since 1846. Accommodation became less cramped due to the erection of additional buildings and fever sheds.

Table No. 33: Recorded child mortality as a percentage of all recorded child admissions calculated from the minute books of Cork union workhouse.

Date	1845	1846	1847	1849	1850	1851
Child Mortality	216	384	1,381	701	585	726
Child Admissions	1,612	5,449	3,337	5,664	6,568	5,939
Percentage	14	7	42	12	9	12

The impact of the famine continued through 1849. The severity of the natural disaster was replaced with the malign influence of the cholera epidemic in the spring and summer months. Girls under fifteen appear to have been less threatened by death in 1849, with 195 female deaths in comparison to 290 male deaths and 216 deaths among infants. The incidence of the cholera cases were higher among the male sex generally according to the reports of Dr Popham and Dr O'Connor. In their last report to the guardians 'of April 20th there occurred in this union workhouse 173 new cases of Asiatic Cholera, viz. 99 males and 74 females … the type of the disease is as yet of a very malignant character running its course with great rapidity'.[19] This explains the greater number of male child deaths as both the adult male and boys wards were in close proximity to each other. A report by the workhouse schoolmaster asserted his belief that the location of the schoolrooms retarded the spread of cholera. 'The cholera still remains confined to the upper part of the western end of the building, none of the school as yet has been attacked. The schoolroom being on the ground floor, thus affording a curious example of an apparently uncertain march of the disease.'[20] By 1850 a change had occurred and this change exhibited a higher number of female deaths, 209 girls died in comparison to 162 boys between the ages of two and fifteen. Age categories in the minute books were altered, with the exception of the category of infants less than two years of age.

Infants under two years displayed little resistance to disease and death. Their immune systems were unable to cope with workhouse diseases resulting from inadequate nutrition and continuous exposure to the stagnant air. In ten months 216 infants died. The figure for 1850 echoed that of 1849 with 214 infant deaths. The frequency of death abated after 1851, when 312 infants died. Arnott lists the mortality statistics for the years 1852 to 1859:

Table No. 34: Mortality amongst infants under two years (1852–59)

1852	1853	1854	1855	1856	1857	1858	1859
232	154	185	167	109	66	102	51

Table 34 derived from Arnott's figures, illustrates a reduction in the instances of death within the infant category. By 1859 there were 51 annual infant deaths.

Table No. 35: Child mortality under the age of 15[21]

1852	1853	1854	1855	1856	1857	1858	1859
626	410	412	310	254	129	152	80

In analysing child mortality table 36 lists the numbers and percentages of all recorded deaths that comprised child deaths:

Table No. 36: Recorded child mortality as a percentage of all recorded deaths calculated from the minute books of the Cork union workhouse:

	1845	1846	1847	1849	1850	1851
Child Mortality	216	384	1381	701	585	726
Total Mortality	486	880	2622	1609	1319	1550
Percentage	44	44	53	44	44	47

From 1845 to 1851 child mortality was between 44 and 53 per cent of all recorded deaths within the Cork union workhouse. In 1845 child mortality accounted for 44 per cent of all workhouse deaths. The impact of the potato failures during the autumn and winter of 1845 increased the tide of admissions into the workhouse. In 1846 the numbers of admissions increased but child mortality accounted for 7 per cent of all child admissions. This figure increased in 1847 to 42 per cent and is reflected in the above table, child mortality as a percentage of total workhouse deaths reached 53 per cent in 1847. The younger generation of workhouse residents, with their underdeveloped immunity, were a vulnerable host for every sort of disease.

Their immune systems were obviously still weak in 1851 when the number of child deaths reached 47 per cent. Although the worst excesses of the famine were over, the number of child deaths continued to increase. As mentioned earlier, one effect of the famine conditions and diseases was their propensity to strike women with more frequency. Consequently it increased the number of orphans and foundlings in long term care. Child mortality figures as a percentage of all recorded death figures increased in 1851 due to continuous tide of child admissions.

An overview of child mortality reveals it was the infant category that suffered the most. Many deaths were of newly born infants. They were born into the institutional culture where the destitute rule was applied to all inmates including children. Their famine experience was described as a house akin to a 'chamber of horrors'.[22] The reality of the famine experience overwhelmed the happiness for the new workhouse mothers. They knew that life expectancy for a newly-born infant was dismal in an atmosphere of contagion and excessive overcrowding. Their harsh realisation was echoed by Arnott, 'for the young child admission to the workhouse was an entrance to the grave'.[23]

In examining the numbers of famine births within the workhouse three noticeable patterns emerged. Firstly, in the initial years 1845 and 1846, the number of female births is higher than male births. Secondly, in 1847 the pattern is altered slightly. Thirdly, in the latter years of the famine the male births surpassed female births. In 1845 there were 79 workhouse births and 120 births were recorded in the minute books of 1846. By then famine had gripped the country and the number of expectant mothers admitted to workhouses increased.

Table No. 37: Workhouse births for 1845, 1846 and 1847 (6 months)

	1845	1846	1847
Female births	43	74	44
Male births	36	46	43

Table No. 38: Recorded workhouse births for 1847 to 1850

	1847 (6 months)	1849 (10 months)	1850
Female births	44	61	77
Male births	43	64	78

The urge to apply for relief to the workhouse was motivated by the prospect of clothing, shelter and meagre food rations together with maternal hopes that they would give their new-born infants a better chance of survival rather than remaining outside the house. The rise in the number of births from 79 to 120 is attributable to increased admissions. Focusing on the summer months of 1845 and 1846 the number of births declined. In the summer months of 1845 the famine was relatively unknown.

For the same period in 1846, the numbers are consistent with those for 1845 (see table 39). Although the numbers of admissions rose overall, they were always reduced in the summer season together with increased discharges.

Table No. 39: Recorded workhouse births, 1845–50

Workhouse births	1845	1846	1847	1849	1850
Jan.	5	12	19		9
Feb.	4	3	28		16
Mar.	8	12	12	12	10
Apr.	12	16	9	13	17
May	7	14	12	22	28
June	5	8	7	23	16
July	5	3		19	13
Aug.	8	6		13	11
Sept.	6	7		8	8
Oct.	3	7		7	6
Nov.	10	16		5	13
Dec.	6	16		3	8
Total	79	120	87	125	155
Average per month	6	10	14	12	13

Note: *omissions occur where the minute book for the respective period is not available.*

The instances of workhouse births increased in March and April. It suggests that children were conceived in the summer months. November and December 1846 shows increased births, attributable perhaps to climatic factors. Winter forced more women to seek admission to the workhouse. Inside the policy of segregation of the sexes was enforced, even amongst married persons. Also the second crop failure in the autumn of 1846 heightened the demand for workhouse accommodation.

From the 1845 figures, 55 per cent of all workhouse births were girls. There were 79 births in total of which 36 were boys and 43 were girls. In 1846, 74 female births accounted for 62 per cent of all workhouse births. For the six-month period January to June 1847 there were 44 female and 43 male births. Calculation of the birth figures in 1849 (based on the ten-month period March to December 1849 as the earlier minute book is missing) indicate that there were 61 female births and 64 male births, constituting 49 and 51 per cent of recorded births respectively. The scenario was replicated in 1850 with 77 female and 78 male births.

The severity of the famine conditions and the increased proliferation of disease and pestilence distinguish the years 1845–1850 into two groups. 1845 and 1846 were the years of recurrent potato failures and starvation. From 1847 to 1850, in addition to starvation, the inmates experienced the typhus, dysentery and cholera epidemics and escalating fatalities.

Associated with the welfare of children is the welfare of the expectant mother. The workhouse also performed the function of a lying-in hospital for pregnant women. The registers detail instances of pregnant women seeking refuge in the house. The lying-in department was recommended for special consideration in 1846 because of its cleanliness and the genuine kindness of its staff. Catherine Hayes was singled out for exceptional conduct in May 1846. As a deputy-nurse tender the visiting committee were alerted to her humanity by the workhouse physicians. The committee duly presented their recommendations that she 'be appointed full nurse tender and receive the same pay, rations and allowances as these servants' of the house. She was to be rewarded for her 'conduct for humanity, care and attention and cleanliness'.[24] Despite the limitations of the poor law, such accounts reflect favourably, on the staff.

Reports in the minutes concerning the paediatric welfare of the workhouse children form two distinct categories. The first category relates to dietary and medical requirements. The second is the institutional social culture that emphasised child accommodation arrangements and workhouse schooling. Inextricably linked with the children's diets were childhood illnesses. They were perceived as just childhood ailments. They often progressed into a more sinister or life-threatening state when left untreated. The institutional culture of the workhouse, its regulations and accommodation arrangements contributed to the spread of disease and an increase in fatalities.

The consignment of children to Cork workhouse was 'an entrance to the grave'.[25] As outlined earlier child fatalities were always between 44 and 53 per cent of total workhouse fatalities. The underlying reasons that accelerated the pace of death among the younger pauper class are many and diverse. Excessive overcrowding, unsanitary conditions and the constant waft of contagious air all imposed upon the frailty of health of the young inmates. Those illnesses prevalent among children upon admission were often similar to those experienced by adult inmates. From the indoor registers those diseases and ailments which were most common to children were opthalamia, skin inflammations, redness in the face, scurvy, scrofula, digestive problems and sore limbs. Nutritional deficiencies prior to admission contributed to the proliferation of these ailments. However an analysis of the house dietary ration illustrates that the workhouse diet itself was so inferior that it metamorphosed the common ailment into an illnesses of deathly proportion.

Such radical changes usually occurred after admission. The incubation periods of the diseases varied from a few days to a week or to six months in the case of scurvy. For the officers at the admission gates there was no method of deciphering which cases would become highly contagious or were potentially fatal.

For many children it was not direct starvation that accelerated death but often the failure of a weak digestive system to actually cope with food and nutrition. Seamus Riordan reminisces on the deathly consequences of food on a delicate constitution: 'The poorhouse in Bandon was soon full of sick and starving people. Deaths were reported by the score ... a meal given to some quite often because their stomachs were so weak from long fasting that solid food was only poison to them'.[26]

The nutritional quality of the diet provided by the Poor Relief Act was, at times, more prejudicial to the health of children than actual starvation. Milk and Indian meal particularly aggravated the children's constitutions. Adequate culinary practices and hygienic preparation of food in the workhouse kitchen were minimal. Cooking times were not adhered to and wheaten foodstuffs were inadequately softened and virtually indigestible.

Indian meal was the principal ingredient in the dietary staple commonly called stirabout. Indian meal was brought into the country under the Peel administration. Large quantities were stored and subsequently used in March 1846. These early imports were old, dry and of an inferior quality and were more difficult to mill. It required pre-soaking and long boiling to soften it to a digestible state. Children who ate such meal suffered intestinal discomfort and at worst hard grains punctured the stomach walls.[27]

The famine menu varied little to that which was devised at the time of the establishment of the union in 1840, the only change being the replacement of potatoes with increased portions of stirabout and meal. The English workhouse diet was similar. In the course of the famine the English dietary outstripped its Irish counterpart. This shows that even the impact of the famine did not deter the guardians from strictly adhering to the cost-conscious policies of the poor law.

Dietary guidelines were established in 1840. The diet of 1842 exhibited a slight modification in the ration of bread for supper. Children's dietary consisted of three categories; children above five and under thirteen years, children aged two to five years, and infants under two years. Children in this latter category were re-

garded as 'those at nurse' and additional rations of milk were provided for toddlers.[28] The older children aged two to thirteen received a diet of potatoes, bread, milk and oatmeal in varying quantities according to age.

Those in the category aged five to thirteen years received four
ounces of oatmeal and half a pint of milk for breakfast three days a
week and two pounds of inferior quality potatoes and the same of
milk for the remainder of the week. The famine was responsible
for this change. During 1845–1849 the potato breakfast was replaced with larger quantities of bread and oatmeal. Milk and two
and a half pounds of potatoes constituted dinner for the children.
Children and adults received a soup-like meal with bread cuttings.
This soup was extremely cost effective and was ordained as nutritious. In reality it was of little value.

The effects of the famine on children's constitutions and high
child mortality did not encourage the guardians to discontinue the
famine dietary. It was all too easy to lay culpability on the 'season
of scarcity', believing that the dietary did not influence diseases or
fatalities.[29] Arnott claims that the workhouse children in 1857 saw
'carogues floating in their soup'.[30] His initial response was disbe-
lief. Following his discoveries of squalor and inferior food he believed the incident of carogues to be very real.[31] Dr Townsend tes-
tified that diseases were generated in the house through inferior
dietary and the dietary as it stood then in 1857 'would in my
opinion not keep them (children) in vigorous health. On the contrary it would reduce their bodies into that state that they would
easily become the victims to disease'.[32] This inferior diet was issued
to all unions in February 1849. It was a response to the modification
of the workhouse diet that occurred in the previous years. It allowed
for greater portions of bread and more soup.

If these were Dr Townsend's deductions in 1857 then the medical officers of the famine period were either lax in their respon-
sibilities or their attempts to ameliorate the condition of the children did not go far enough to combat the famine menace. Under
the 1846 Fever Act physicians were made responsible for inmate
welfare and dietary arrangements. The existing diet continued to

be the bill of fare for all except those whom Dr O'Connor deemed in need of additional rations for medical reasons.

The minutes list numerous references to the supply of inferior quality milk and bread by contractors to the workhouse. In these instances Dr O'Connor (acting under the auspices of the Fever Act) drew the house committee's attention to the quality of milk and bread. He recognised the threat contaminated or inferior quality milk posed to infants and children. 'The infant children require more nutritious food than at present supplied, that the skimmed milk through boiling on delivery becomes sour an hour afterwards'.[33] Dr O'Connor and the house committee recognised the shortcomings of the workhouse diet. The guardians were loath to change despite the worsening crisis. Some weeks after Dr O'Connor's suggestion regarding the infants' milk, it was decided to terminate Mr Reed's contract for the supply of milk to the house.[34] The board's reluctance to change contractors could be perceived as an element of misanthropy and an adherence to cost efficiency whereby the milk supplies previously tendered were the cheapest available.

In reality the guardians were unable to deal with the crisis adhering to their primary functions of admitting and classifying paupers. Adherence to workhouse rules signified that the dietary requirements of infants and children were low on the guardians' list of priorities. The guardians were under pressure in executing their duties. A report to the poor law commissioners detailed their grievances as regards staffing, underpayment and overcrowding. It acknowledged that 'Cork workhouse houses more inmates than those of the two Dublin houses and that the duties of the Cork house are immeasurably greater than those of the two Dublin houses combined'.[35]

In such conditions it is hardly surprising that little attention was given to the requirements of the younger paupers. However the diet for children in English workhouses was more favourable than the Irish diet at any time either before or after the famine. Prior to the famine the destitute rule could be used as its defence. However the lowest class of an English pauper was still higher than that of its Irish counterpart, for this reason their diet to an extent was more nutritious.

In a case study of two English workhouses in Cheshire and Norfolk the children's diet was more diverse. Children received bread, gruel, potatoes and broth in similar quantities to the Cork dietary. In contrast they received cooked meat and bacon four times a week. Gressenhall workhouse diet in Norfolk was more favourable in its paediatric diet in 1838 than Cork workhouse. Children under nine were dieted at discretion; those over nine were allowed the same quantities as able-bodied women. Similar to Northwich workhouse the diet also included 12 ounces of meat pudding and vegetables, suet pudding and weekly rations of butter and cheese.[36] The Cork dietary was monotonous and deficient in nutritional value thus impairing the health of the children.

Potatoes were a rich source of carbohydrate and vitamins, especially vitamin C, for the pauper classes. Prolonged absence of vitamin C contributed to a wide variety of childhood diseases. Opthalamia, excessive dryness of the eyeball, particularly affected children. The indoor register for 1848–50 cites a proliferation of ophthalmic cases amongst children at admission. The institutional culture of the house together with contaminated milk and water was conducive to the spread of this disease.

The sleeping arrangements in the children's quarters meant between three and five children slept in a bed. The situation in April 1840 saw 'four schoolboys sleep in a bed of three feet broad and six feet long, girls sleep five in bed'.[37] With the onslaught of overcrowding in the famine period and the failure of the house capacity to increase accordingly, these arrangements became more 'injurious to the health' of children.[38]

Infants under two years had the highest propensity to contract fever and dysentery. Their low resistance and diet, mainly of milk, which was frequently of an inferior quality and left exposed, acted as an agent in spreading these virulent diseases. Children and adults alike used communal washing facilities. The sanitary facilities and cesspools were exposed and frequently inmates including boys above nine were employed in the maintenance of these. Given that much disease was spread through contaminated water and insects, it is easy to conceive of a high mortality among children. Disease, however, was not generated solely in the workhouse.

Much disease entered undetected upon admission of inmates as the symptoms were slight. The indoor registers refer to skin conditions, sore legs, sore hands, itch and red faces, which in appearance seemed non-life threatening but were fatal. Erysipelas, a highly contagious and infectious disease that attacks skin tissues, was often characterised by a red face, nose or butterfly-shaped blotches on the face. The aged, infirm and the infants were most likely to contract erysipelas. Newly-born infants were especially vulnerable through the exposure of their umbilical tissues.

Those children complaining of sore limbs often were sometimes exhibiting the initial stages of scurvy. A complete lack of vitamin C requires six months to develop into scurvy. Those that entered the house with scurvy surely died as the house diet included no fruit and only a semblance of vegetables in the soup.

Epidemic typhus commonly called famine fever or jail fever was especially recurrent in highly populated institutions. Non-observation of adequate sanitation and hygiene practices in congested wards led to the escalation of this louse borne disease. Typhus claimed between 50 and 70 per cent of those affected. Two types of typhus were found in the workhouse, the relapsing type (referred to as yellow fever) which generally was contracted by a person who had survived the first attack and the epidemic type which was in the majority of cases fatal. Usually the fever was preceded by scurvy.[39] For children and infants the typhus epidemics of 1846 and 1847 were their first exposures to this disease. This accounts for the high mortality rates among infants under two years and explains why child deaths accounted for 53 per cent of all workhouse deaths in 1847. Adolescents were frequently attacked and females more regularly than males.[40] Dr Lalor, the physician to Kilkenny workhouse, in his paper to the Royal College of Surgeons on the 1846 fever epidemic, noted that the old and young were most susceptible to typhus fever. From his case notes he clearly found that the children put up a greater fight against the fever. 'One child possessed of more stamina held out until the forty-eight day'.[41] As with other famine diseases, close physical contact, the sleeping arrangements, lack of isolation during the actual disease and the incubation periods contributed to its rampage through the workhouse.

In conclusion, paediatric health and general welfare were severely curtailed by the famine since it altered the usual food source and stretched the habitation arrangements in the workhouse. Dr Popham, graphically outlined the factors which were prejudicial to health:

> deficient and bad food, intemperate habits, neglect of personal cleanliness, and the effluvia accumulated from numbers herded together like gregarious animals, in ill ventilated buildings… the evil effects of overcrowding were fatally evident in the workhouses during the famine, showing that of all the auxiliaries to health, pure air is that which can be least neglected with impunity.[42]

One area of child welfare that was not neglected was the area of education. Education in the workhouse incorporated two aspects. It focused not only on ordinary children but attempted to cater for children with disabilities. The registers describe some of the children entering the workhouse as 'deaf and dumb'. These children were placed under the care of Dr Kehoe.

Dr Patrick Kehoe was a physician with an address at Cook Street.[43] He was also the treasurer of the Cork School for Deaf and Dumb Children. Children with such a disability were not allowed attend the workhouse school but special provision to educate them at Dr Kehoe's school was made. The Cork guardians resolved that he 'receive for the education of deaf mutes the sum of £6 per annum'.[44] One such pauper was the daughter of Julia Hunt (inmate), who was seven years old and it was decided that 'she be sent to Dr Kehoe's school for deaf and dumb children'.[45] The incident illustrated the guardians' willingness to offer as much attention as then affordable to children with disabilities but also it reiterated their stance that they were primarily an institution dedicated to the alleviation of distress. Julia Hunt's daughter was lucky, she experienced the 'kindness' of the guardians whilst avoiding the worst horrors of the famine experience in the workhouse.

Children in the workhouse attended the workhouse school and received a basic education. The poor law regime intended that all children receive an education, however meagre. It would increase their job prospects and allow them to become suitable emigrants, educated in the basic skills of reading, writing and arithmetic. In schooling arrangements segregation also existed, the boys were separated from the girls. In addition to hours spent in the schoolrooms both sexes worked in the various workhouse departments. The girls served what the workhouse staff termed 'apprenticeships' in the sewing and spinning rooms, while the boys were apprenticed to the male inmates working in the tailoring, shoemaking, carpentry and weaving departments.

The issue of workhouse education could be cited as one area that the famine did not significantly impact upon. The trends of extending the number of operational workhouse schools and the attendance rolls continued in the course of the famine. Workhouse schools came under the remit of the National Board of Education in Dublin. The thirteenth report of the education board under Section IV stated that at the end of 1846 there existed ninety-nine workhouse schools, an increase of nine on the previous year.[46] One of the issues raised was that of apprenticeships. Apprenticeships were already underway in the workhouse departments, but the commissioners envisaged a system whereby they would receive a more technical education and commented thus on the workhouse schools; 'any system of mere literary instruction pursued by [pauper children] would in itself be incomplete, the majority are deprived of guardianship by their parents ... [and] the intention of transferring each pupil at the proper stage of advancement to the industrial establishments, similar to Norwood School in England'.[47]

Also under discussion in the report was inadequate payment for workhouse teachers. Often they were reliant on voluntary contributions and many teachers preferred to take other employment rather than teach in a workhouse school. To remedy this scenario it was decided to establish a board of superintendents who would 'award annual gratuities to the most deserving of the workhouse teachers' to entice them to work.[48]

At the time of the report the school-master at Cork workhouse was in receipt of £7-10-0 per quarter.[49] Salaries for educational staff remained unchanged in 1848.[50] The famine however contributed to a financial impact on the salaries of workhouse teachers. Since the early years of Cork workhouse the payments to teachers had deceased. During the famine years the strained financial situation could not afford to increase their salaries. In 1842 the schoolmaster and mistress were paid £30 and £25 respectively.[51] The account books always display a gender difference.

Despite the lack of teachers in the workhouses it was undeniable that many children received an education, however basic, during the famine. The institutional culture in the educational area was beneficial, as pauper children's attendance at parochial schools at the height of the famine would have been doubtful. The following table based on 1853 figures illustrates the success of the workhouses schooling during the famine.[52]

Table No. 40: Literacy levels among children and young adults

	9 to 15 years	15 to 21 years
Can neither read nor write	13.1%	40.3%
Read and write	39.3%	21.9%

In the age category nine to fifteen years only 13.1 per cent of children could neither read nor write, this positively reflects that 86.9 per cent in those in this age category had some literacy skills. The table reflects that the younger paupers had perhaps more consistent education. Many in this age category in 1853 would have been between one and eight years at the onset of the famine and hence received their immediate education in the workhouse. Those in the category fifteen to twenty-one years were aged between seven and thirteen in 1845 and would have had little education until their workhouse schooling. This is evident again in the younger group as they were more literate at an earlier age with

39.3 per cent able to read and write in 1853.

In conclusion it is obvious that death, disease and the very nature of the institution marred workhouse children, both physically and psychologically. The workhouse had its faults and failings but it was funded on scanty resources and inadequate staffing arrangements. It should be noted that the guardians and staff were not devoid of humanity. Many in fact failed to cope with the stresses of their daily routines during the famine and afforded what compassion as they could to all victims, perhaps most especially the children of the house whilst at all times adhering to the policies that governed their working environment.

5

INSTITUTIONAL CULTURE

Appoint one chief commissioner …
Five hundred guardians vice and volunteer,
Five hundred clerks at fifty pounds a year …
Five hundred health board doctors of all names …
'The Inheritor and the Economist'[1]

Many writers on the famine allude to the overriding bureaucratic
nature of the poor law. The institutional landscape of the house
was far from that of the bureaucratic relief provider. Beyond bureaucracy, the workhouse represented a microcosm of society and as
such the administrators of the house performed various disciplinary and arbitrary roles. These roles included those of judge, jury,
law maker and enforcer, moral and religious co-ordinator, and on
occasions, facilitator of assisted passages and grantor of marriage
licences. It also incorporated the notion that the workhouse was
akin to a prison system, 'the English Bastile (union workhouse) is
seen as a product of two types of power which are characteristic of
modern societies; one associated with administration (government) and the other with institutions (discipline)'.[2]

Discipline and administration were inextricably linked. The
administration of the workhouse, the house regulations and the
daily routines outlined the poor law commissioners' agenda to
establish discipline amongst paupers. Poor law discipline had many
facades and the idea of subjugating Irish paupers was a function of
overall poor law policy. The workhouse was represented as a disciplinary institution, whereby the specific characteristics of the
Irish pauper mentality as identified by Nicholl's would be controlled. The disciplinary agenda reflected a penological policy
whereby:

the poor law authorities represented the workhouse as a place where discipline reigned, rather than the caprice of individuals, an institution whose inmates and officials were impressed above all with the power of rule.[3]

Such ideals were not designed with criminals in mind but in this case, however, it sufficed to act as a deterrent for those seeking admission to the house. Perceptions of the workhouse portray it as a correctional institution. Its objectives as a correctional institution covered many facets of workhouse life. Correctional objectives were primarily evident in the areas of house regulations and in the nature of the work provided for inmates in various departments which was laborious and at times hazardous to the younger and malnourished inmates. The institutional culture of the house in terms of its educational and religious functions was not only correctional but also impressed the idea of morality upon the Irish paupers.

The 'moral geometry' of the house as referred to by Felix Driver was clearly seen in the separation of the sexes and the classes in all workhouses.[4] House regulations and segregation of the lower classes were the vehicles for translating this sense of morality to all inmates. How then did workhouse regulations instil a sense of morality and achieve their correctional ambitions? The regulations and the physical dimensions of the house were based on spatial separation.

It segregated the sexes, identified classes of pauperism and classified inmates according to age and ability, while the layout of the house into yards and wards accommodated separation. The commissioners' workhouse rules order in 1842 stated that a 'ward or separate building or yard should be assigned to each class of pauper' hence rendering them 'without communication with those of any other class'.[5]

Spatial separation served three functions. It allowed for the appropriate treatment of inmates. This was evident in the areas of diet and work, which were organised according to age and ability. Secondly, it was used as a deterrent to pauperism. In keeping paupers separate it was hoped they would be weaned away from their impoverished lifestyle, reflecting the belief that paupers were responsible for their own destitution. Separation from family and friends was seen as an incentive for paupers to improve their lot by embracing the educational and correctional facilities provided in the workhouse. Thirdly, it was to provide a barrier to the moral and physical contagion of the house. In areas of physical contagion spatial separation was ineffective.[6] The actual functioning of these guiding principles for spatial separation during the famine must be closely scrutinised.

The French correspondent Gustave de Beaumont said of the workhouse system that 'with one hand they offered the poor an alms, with the other they offered a prison'.[7] Paupers seeking admission were scrutinised for correction. Once admitted, the workhouse targeted those inmates who transgressed regulations and committed crimes. Crime in Cork workhouse was mainly a reaction to the institutional environment. Crimes committed in the workhouse consisted largely of offences against property. Inmates caused deliberate damage to property in an attempt to expose their grievances. An examination of inmate crime during the famine period verifies this.

House officials too occasionally faltered under the pressure of events, committing offences against house policy. The punishments handed down to deviant inmates and staff were severe. Compounded with decrepit physiological conditions it was far from humane. Workhouse policy advanced the notion that Irish paupers were culpable for their own destitution and transgression of regulations brought severe, even inhumane, retribution. The master of the workhouse had a punishment book for the misbehaviour of inmates. He was the person empowered to administer punishment to any pauper for any of the following misbehaviours (figure 18). Punishment often caused widespread resentment and often resulted in further disturbances.

Fig. No. 18: List of Misbehaviours[8]

    Making unnecessary noise
    Obscene language
    Insulting behaviour

Assault
Refusal to work
Refusal to comply with workhouse regulations
Gaming
Smoking and possession of tobacco
Possession of alcohol
Disturbance during religious practice
Absconding from the workhouse
Feigning illness
Disobedience of workhouse officers

The actual nature of workhouse crime was often akin to minor disturbances and misdemeanours. Inmates need not be criminals to be perceived as such. They reportedly exhibited a semblance of criminal habits in their disregard for workhouse law and order and their consecutive offences. Inmates rebelled for three succinct reasons. Firstly, they protested in the hope that the poor law authorities would introduce better accommodation arrangements. Secondly, punishment from the guardians could see them lodged in the gaol with its promise of better diet and conditions. Thirdly, transportation, despite its inherent risks, could appear favourable to the desperate inmate.

Social disruption as a result of the potato failures increased the instances of crime throughout the country not least in the workhouses. As admissions increased and capacity became strained instances of workhouse crime escalated. Helen Litton estimates the rise in overall crime during the famine increased from

> 20,000 on trial in 1845 to nearly 39,000 in 1849, was mainly due to non-violent crimes against property, not against persons … the most common crime was theft of food and clothing but many of the large numbers arrested died before they could be brought to trial … as the famine worsened people began to commit crimes deliberately so they might be transported, however dreadful it might be it could not be worse than dying from starvation or fever where they were.[9]

According to Cooke and Scanlon, 'the prison system seemed to hold more attraction for them and as a result crimes were committed frequently to gain access, in prisons at least there they could be sure of a bed and of food'.[10]

Workhouses were institutions that afforded a basic existence to those who qualified for relief as they met the terms of the 'destitute rule'. Those who gained admission under false pretences were expelled from the house once their deception was uncovered. A male inmate guilty of desertion was expelled automatically from the workhouse and ordered to maintain his kin by work or receive one month's hard labour plus imprisonment. Inmates were incarcerated usually in the infamous 'black hole'. The 'notorious black hole has been described as a dark space, eight feet long by ten feet high and six feet wide and many are believed to have starved to death' when compounded with a period of reduced rations whilst in confinement.[11] Confinement in such a place of weak, starving inmates was harsh and an obvious example of the extent to which the poor law authorities would go to instil discipline and deter destitution.

A sentence of hard labour was usually associated with difficult menial work such as breaking stones. More often it was administered using a device called a Perrott Wheel which was operated by up to one hundred inmates.[12] Inmates guilty of an offence were compelled to work this device for longer, more exhaustive periods. It was work without incentive or motivation, yet fulfilled the fundamental rule of the workhouse system – that no one capable of work should be idle. The Perrott Wheel, designed by Richard Perrott of Cork, was accepted by the commissioners 'for use in the workhouses as a means of keeping large numbers of workers employed simultaneously'. Beyond its purpose for grinding corn it was a punitive device. Compelling inmates to operate the wheel was deemed 'objectionable and inhumane and its use was discontinued after the famine'.[13]

Inmates were forbidden to smoke tobacco or to have any alcoholic beverages in their possession unless expressly sanctioned by the house physician. 'Bad language, malingering, waste and disobedience were to be punished by confinement and reduced rations'.[14] These rules were justifiable in an environment where bedding consisted of straw and timber and where raucous behaviour could escalate into uncontrollable riots given the volume of people in the workhouse. Similarly, card games and 'all games of chance were forbidden and the master was entitled to confiscate such items'.[15] Either the porter or the master supervised the once weekly visitation of inmates thus further reinforcing the penal nature of the workhouse.

Inmate offences can be categorised into offences against property, absconding from the house and cases of falsified admission. Levels of workhouse crime are examined in two distinct phases. These phases look at crimes committed during the period September 1845 to April 1846, and thereafter until 1850. [The minutes for the period July 1847 to March 1849 are missing.] An examination of crime in each of these periods illustrates the impact of the famine on the mentality of inmates. More importantly the examination for the second phase from May 1846 to June 1847 and March 1849 to January 1850 denotes the impact of the famine experience on staff and house officials, as they too succumbed to the urge to commit offences against the institution.

In the first phase the majority of crimes were committed by male inmates and consisted largely of offences against property and falsification of status to gain access to the workhouse. There are numerous instances of the phrase 'discharged being "fit" objects'.[16] The theft of union clothing during an escape from the house constituted an offence against workhouse property. Inmates were readily identified by the legend of the Cork union and their inmate numbers, both of which were visible on the uniform. Captured inmates upon their return faced punishment for absconding while wearing the workhouse property. Such infractions were dealt with harshly and the punishment doled out consisted of hard labour, solitary confinement or expulsion from the workhouse.

In October 1845 the master of the house reported that he had apprehended Francis Gregory and John Crowley in the process of 'making away with several yards of frieze, the property of the contractor and that the fabric was subsequently found concealed in several places having been cut into several pieces'.[17] The minutes do not cite the punishment they received but the minutes of the previous week allude to a conspiracy between the men and women.

Although communication was forbidden between the sexes, it is probable that the female dressmaking department and the male tailoring departments colluded. On 4 October 1845, 'Catherine O'Doherty and Catherine Carthy have been detected in cutting up house clothing and converting them into bodices with the purpose of selling them'.[18] The clerk did not qualify this incident with additional details of punishment or subsequent actions of these women.

Such actions were precipitated by the failure of the potato harvest and the need to accrue funds to purchase more rations The once weekly visits from the outside could have facilitated the sale of these purloined garments. They took advantage of their employment to obtain additional clothing for themselves, given that all pauper clothing was removed from their possession upon entry and their only articles of clothing were the union uniform. These incidents were reported in early October, inmates believing that their tattered uniforms would not be adequate for the approaching winter. Whether motivated by profit or desperation the offenders' actions underline the depravity of their situation.

The clerk's accounts of such crimes in the years 1845–46 were cursory. For the week ended 18 April the clerk referred to absconding inmates simply as 'the four who deserted with the clothing belonging to the house'.[19] They were duly sentenced to hard labour but were also to be whipped. Corporal punishment was widely extolled as conducive to good discipline. The guardians referred to corporal punishment in the minutes as 'a sentence calculated to improve the morals of those sent for trial from the workhouse'.[20]

During the same week in April 1846 seven other desertees were arrested and re-housed in the Cork workhouse 'and information was sworn against them'.[21] The reference to informants gives cause for speculation. In recording these incidents the clerk omitted a lot of pertinent details, not least the names of both inmates and informants in addition to the nature of their apprehension by union officials. The ward master or mistress in the course of their patrols most likely reported the disappearance of the inmates. A ward master or mistress was assisted in his or her policing duties by a system of rewarding inmates who passed information to the workhouse officials. Such assistance by fellow inmates saw them receive supplementary rations. Under such depraved circumstances as accompanied the famine period, it can be assumed that some inmates informed on others purely in an attempt to survive and secure additional food.

Donnelly cites 1846 as the year in which, 'the criminal business [of the country] came to consist almost entirely of offences against property fuelled by want and hunger'.[22] 1846 witnessed an escalation of workhouse crime in Cork. A majority of the perpetrators were female reflecting the greater number of female to male admissions. Records for May 1846 list four females who were tried and convicted for destruction of workhouse property. Margaret Williams destroyed a cloak, shawl and an apron whereas the trio of Catherine Kelly, Mary Kearney and Hanora Goulden broke glass. These reports are characteristic of the reports of the clerk; he cites their names, qualifies their crime with the punishment received, but omits to detail their convictions or the particular offence.

The rise in crime at this time was largely attributable to the increasing admissions and the congestion amongst the inmates. Donnelly notes that, 'Cork City received the brunt of desperate migration beginning in October 1846 and the influx during the last two months, were from all parts of the county, were overwhelming'.[23] After October 1846 workhouse crime was not so confined to inmates but it came to include staff members also. Consecutive crop failures and increased admissions constantly reinforced the desperation evident outside the workhouse. Staff, who on a daily basis were confronted by such abject misery too, often succumbed to criminal impulses.

Staff transgressions were essentially breaches of house policy as opposed to destructive impulses. Nevertheless the guardians dealt them with in an equally rigorous manner. The guardians frowned on staff transgressions as an ultimate betrayal of their duty to help inaugurate 'a new era in public life when the prevalence of official impartiality, efficiency, economy and standardised and scientific methods of administration would raise the moral tone of the whole community'.[24] In July 1846 Wardmaster Chadwick resigned after the master reported him to the board of guardians.[25] In the proceedings there is a noticeable absence of detail of Chadwick's purported offence. This paucity of detail contrasts with an earlier entry of January 1845, where copious detail is provided in defence of the master's reputation. In a letter read to the board by the clerk of the union the master sought the assistance of the chaplains in the discharge of his duties which had become irksome and difficult with increased admissions. He stated that his 'efforts to maintain order and discipline were paralysed by the opposition given to him, Gentlemen – he has been portrayed as an arbitrary tyrant ... he trusts that the board will excuse him for protesting against the assumed right of others to whom no such authority has been given'.[26]

Staff transgressions and complaints were few until the later year of 1849. The reactions of the workhouse staff and officers to the horrors of the post-1847 environment are apparent. In these later years the minutes frequently record cases of alcohol abuse – nurses, bakers, schoolmistress and other house officials allegedly being under the influence and negligent in the performance of their duties. The female employees were most culpable. During the week of 12 May 1849 the master reported that a nurse was found to be tipsy at nine o'clock in the hospital when on duty. For this she was fined a fortnight's salary.[27]

Cholera was rampant throughout Cork workhouse in May 1849 and one of the remedies applied by the workhouse physicians were alcoholic stimulants. The workhouse provisions lists included orders for porter and whiskey at that time.[28] The medical profession held that whiskey assisted in alleviating the suffering of cholera victims. The volume of alcohol available to hospital staff offered the dual temptations of inebriation and potential immunity from cholera. Witnessing death, disease and despair could not but take its toll on the employees of the house. The baker found solace in alcohol earlier in 1846 when performing his daily duties.

In May he came to work 'intoxicated' and for this 'he was brought before the master for being "tipsy" and consequently dismissed'.[29]

The moral wellbeing of the institution's children was thought to have been endangered by the actions of the schoolmistress. On Sunday night, 6 May 1849, she was found to have kept her husband in the lower house contrary to the master's orders.[30] This breach of house rules emphasises that the poor law policy of separation of classes, sexes and children and the lack of contact between inmates also applied to staff. Staff shortages were an obvious problem for the guardians and there are numerous instances during 1849–50 where healthy inmates were given additional rations to assist house officers in their duties. This was largely the result of a lack of funds to employ further staff and in line with the fiscal restraint policies of the poor law but it also testifies to the increasing number of inmates in the house.

The moral and spiritual welfare of inmates and staff was under the direction of the catholic and protestant chaplains, Reverends Sheehan and Clifford respectively. Father Augustine Maguire was, at one stage Rev. Sheehan's assistant. Throughout the famine years the Convent of Mercy sisters assisted the house clerics in the religious welfare of inmates. From their annals one gets a glimpse of the suffering in the famine stricken workhouse. Their accounts of 1846, are particularly vivid describing the 'dire distress' which dictated that their labours to attend the victims of the workhouse were greatly increased. It is difficult to imagine that these sisters, who usually visited in groups of ten, could adequately provide assistance to inmates numbering over 2,500 during 1846. They spent long hours attending the sick. For the officers of the house they provided much needed assistant nursing staff, and for the inmates their presence and acts of kindness were more beneficial. The Convent of Mercy annals verifies the impact of the famine on mortality. In 1847 'famine fever raged and ten sisters were stricken down with the fever in the early months, out of this number two died'.[31] In the workhouse, religion was tolerated and from the accounts, sectarianism and discrimination appeared to be non-existent.

The poor law by assigning one chaplain to each religious grouping catered for their religious welfare. As with other areas fiscal restraint was apparent here also. The institution was designed to house 2,000 inmates and accordingly there were to be two chaplains with specific functions. When capacity was trebled and inmates numbered up to 7,100 during 1849, there was no consequential increase in the number of administering chaplains. The catholic chaplain Rev. Sheehan was provided temporarily with an assistant curate. Rev. Sheehan was assigned to Cork workhouse in March 1840, and Rev. Clifford was appointed in July of 1840, after the resignation of Rev. Hall of St Nicholas' parish. He had been appointed to the house initially with Rev. Sheehan in March.[32]

As religious co-ordinator for the largest inmate group Rev. Sheehan always received a higher salary than the protestant chaplain. Hired at a salary of £50 per annum, within two months the troublesomeness of his duties secured a rise to £80 per annum. The protestant chaplain's salary remained lower than his catholic counterpart. The catholic cleric received an annual salary of £80 to £85, while Rev. Clifford was in receipt of £45 per annum.[33] Pressurised by the famine the guardians attempted to stretch their resources in other areas and religious salaries remained constant during 1845–1850. The clerk of the union detailed the extent of his many duties. Rev. George Sheehan,

> spends the entire of every Saturday at hearing confessions and of every Sunday in officiating at the mass and in giving religious instruction to the paupers and spends so many hours of every other day on attending the sick and dying as to render his time exclusively engaged in performance of his duties.[34]

In addition to their pastoral duties the chaplains had an official duty to make themselves available to attend board meetings when required by the guardians.[35]

Despite the horrors of starvation and with the urge to survive paramount, a number of marriages took place between the inmates but these were very sporadic. They were sporadic for two succinct reasons. Rev. Sheehan believed that 'persons ought not to marry while in the workhouse' because of the segregation of both parties and the lack of communication and inmates were generally more interested in their fight for survival than to be considering marriage.[36] Rev. Sheehan perceived that workhouse marriages were not practicable, and 'ought to be a rare occurrence. It is my rule to refuse to marry persons while they continue as inmates of this institution'.[37]

Prior to the famine, marriage acts were read before the board but these were only cases in which Rev. Sheehan saw fit to make some exceptions. The rare marriage that occurred during the famine occurred for three reasons. Firstly, an exception was made in the case of a mixed marriage performed in the Established Church and the parties were then seeking a catholic blessing. Secondly, he facilitated marriages in instances where one party was confined and was ill in the workhouse and who desired to marry before imminent death. Thirdly, when marrying couples had accrued the means to survive and were independent of the institution and would leave the workhouse within a day or two, the marriage was performed. During the famine there were approximately one or two marriages per year mentioned in the minute books. However, the duties of the protestant chaplain were substantially less. In the first three years of the institution's operation he performed not a single marriage.

The chaplains' duties were not solely of a religious nature. They often made representations to the guardians on behalf of the inmates and were successful on occasion. One such representation took place in May 1847 when they proposed that additional rations be added to the dietary arrangements. Similarly they took an interest in the emigration of inmates from the workhouse, providing them with prayer books and bibles.[38] Their interest in the sphere of emigration was not solely pastoral, they also acted in an official capacity on behalf of the guardians.

The death toll of the famine reduced the population of the Cork poor law unions by 20 per cent to 36 per cent in the years 1841 to 1851. The reduction was in part attributed to emigration. The colonial land and emigration commission was set up in 1840 in England under the control of the British colonial office. The policy of assisted emigration was established prior to the famine but only became an institutionalised feature after 1845.

Between 1845 and 1851, with an increasing influx of paupers into the workhouse, assisted emigration was an obvious remedy to help reduce the numbers of inmates dependent on poor law relief. Regular circulars brought the availability of emigration to the attention to the boards of guardians. The guardians frequently received such letters that referred to a demand for females of good character for emigration to New South Wales and other destinations.

In Cork workhouse female inmates outnumbered males inmates, usually in the ratio of two to one. With a greater female population such a demand could be facilitated. Subsidised passages were financially expedient. At a cost of between £3 and £5 per emigrant, it was often cheaper to assist inmates to emigrate than allow them to remain and consequently pressurise an already strained poor rate. Emigration presented a 'means for which the rising generation of workhouse inmates could be permanently provided [for]'.[39]

During 1845 and 1846 the official proceedings make few references to cases of assisted emigration from Cork. Generally, inmates who were previously inmates of the house of industry were those singled out for emigration, thereby creating additional vacancies for the destitute paupers. In November 1845 the workhouse emigration committee decided to send to a colony some females who came to the workhouse from the house of industry.[40]

Three months later the committee extolled the virtue of the moderate cost involved (it would not exceed £5 per head) in sending 'a limited number say of fifty young women of good character then resident in the workhouse but late of the house of industry to the Cape of Good Hope'.[41] The expediency of removing these females from the workhouse was such that as much funding as necessary was to be collected to send even more than fifty females. With regard to obtaining finance the reputable services of Rev. Sheehan were employed. He was asked to write to the colonial office to make representations to secure additional funds.

The effect of the famine was clearly demonstrated in the necessity to export paupers to provide additional accommodation within the overcrowded institution. But the general consensus in 1846 suggested that a famine did not exactly exist but the situation was a 'season of scarcity' and with previous crop failures it was anticipated that it would be of a short duration.[42] Although workhouse emigration alleviated the stress of the house its ultimate benefits and problems did not accrue until the later years of 1847 to 1850. According to Donnelly in 1846 a total of 7,066 people emigrated from Cork county and this was superseded in 1847 when the numbers emigrating reached 17,519.[43]

From 1847 the nature of emigration changed and denoted a rise of problems. With so many people wishing to emigrate and since the financial assistance available to them in the workhouse was constantly in demand, a cheaper option was necessary. Emigration to Canada increased. The exodus of 1847 onwards was largely self-perpetuating with remittances being sent to Ireland by relatives and persons who had emigrated in 1845 and 1846. In addition to an increased exodus much of the records detail that menial work placement was available once one emigrated.

In 1848 Richard Dowden, guardian, was in correspondence with a Mr Flour from Stratford-upon-Avon with a view to sending emigrants from Cork workhouse to Shawneentown, Illinois. Mr Flour's brother-in-law was the contact in Illinois. Dowden was furnished with a list of those willing to take emigrants in Shawneentown and that they were to be employed as domestic servants. The letter, dated October 1848, stated that they 'will not only be shielded from want and deprivation but will be received with credible families where they will be justly and kindly treated'.[44] As famine conditions worsened the number of proposals for emigration became more numerous. The outgoing letter book records that in May 1848 200 names were forwarded to the poor law commissioners for assisted 'emigration to Australia'.[45] The minutes for 1848 refer to a demand from the emigration commissioners relating to the shortage of women in Australia. This circular was sent to all unions and it enquired as to the number of young orphaned girls aged between fourteen and eighteen years who could be emigrated. It advocated that costs would be kept to a minimum and that the only costs the union would incur would be their passage to Plymouth.[46]

From 1847 much correspondence took place between Irish and English unions as Irish paupers often fled Ireland to take up residence in English unions. Correspondence between the Northwich union and the poor law commissioners in Dublin in July 1847 testifies that 1847 was by far the worst year of the famine. As evidenced in a letter (see emigration, Appendix 3) temporary accommodation had to be erected to house those suffering from famine fever. In Northwich it preceded the construction of a permanent fever hospital on site.[47] Emigration from Irish workhouses was problematical for the host country.

Any alleviation of overcrowded conditions afforded by emigration was in the case of Cork union often negated by the policy upheld by many English unions, which was to return Irish emigrants to their union of origin. This particularly affected the Cork union. The poor law commissioners wrote to the guardians in February 1846 stating that the destitute Irish in England could be returned home but those English paupers in Ireland could remain. A committee in Cork workhouse asserted their belief, that in the time of distress that a period of residency of three years of an Irishman in England should qualify him for relief under the English poor law. They argued that 'Irishmen who have expended the best portion of their lives in England should in the event of them becoming destitute be forcibly sent home' was completely objectionable.[48] The fragmentary registers testify that elderly inmates were often returned from England or they were British by birth but had spent time in Ireland, as in the case of George Williams, aged 60, and whose occupation was a seaman. Women entering the workhouse cited their husbands as being amongst the emigrants to Bristol, Gloucester, Canada, Sydney, America and Australia and consequently they were deserted.[49]

The famine began the mass exodus of Irish men and women

to foreign shores. An editorial in the *Cork Examiner* in January 1849 emphasised this exodus, 'they fly the land as if a pesthouse and quit the soil of their youth and manhood, as if the demon plague was running riot in the fields'.[50]

Although the figures indicated an exodus, assisted emigration came to feature more in the union ledger account books for the period 1849 and 1850 and later. In the accounts for November 1849 assisted emigration from the city of Cork, its hinterland and the electoral districts, numbered 62 at a total cost of over £200.[51] Six months later in May 1850 emigration from the union was over five times that of the previous November at 333.[52] This was attributed to the fact that the worst was over but discharges were accelerated and discharged inmates had nothing to return to but the prospect of a better life in a different country.

Those who survived their institutional confinement could be grateful for their lives but the guardians cannot be criticised for not going far enough. Faced with limitations on any independent decisions they took, it is best to remember that the presence of these buildings helped to save lives and contributed to the Irish diaspora. Overall the famine impacted greatly upon the institutional environment of the workhouse. In the aftermath of the famine one could describe the institution as 'a prison without the accommodation of a prison, an asylum without the comforts of an asylum and a sick hospital with the special proviso that it was of no proper convenience for sick people', whilst portraying a microcosm or exemplar of Irish pauper society.[53]

CONCLUDING THOUGHTS

The diaspora of Irish emigrants brought their shared famine experiences to Australia, Canada and the United States. Much of the discourse on the famine is of a general nature. This book, specific to Cork union, has sought to examine the impact of the famine within the Cork workhouse and it goes beyond detailing the actual history of the famine, rather it seeks to explore and portray the tragic and significant effects of the famine as they unfolded in Cork city. In doing so it conveys the reality of the most shattering event in Irish history as endured by a local community.

The construction of the workhouse reflected the demographics of the city. Initially the Cork workhouse was adapted from the old house of industry to facilitate a speedy implementation of the poor law in Ireland. At a short distance from the house of industry work commenced on the new purpose built workhouse. It would accommodate 2,000 paupers of the vast and populous union. It opened to receive paupers on 1 March 1840. Costing £12, 800 and another £8,000 for its fitting-out, it was situated on a site measuring 12 acres.

By comparison the metropolis of Dublin had two workhouses, located on the north and south sides of the city. Both of these together in terms of their building costs and their fixtures and fittings were actually less expensive than the Cork house and accommodated 2,000 paupers each. Reduced expenditure was largely due to the fact that these two Dublin workhouses were initially a house of industry and a foundling hospital and they were subsequently adapted to become workhouses.[1] Both opened after Cork union workhouse in April and May 1840 respectively. This comparison serves to highlight that although the appearance of these buildings on the Irish landscape were founded under the same poor law premise and architectural design, their practical application was different in accordance with their regional variance. The individual accounts in the minutes of the Cork union convey the impact of the famine on one particular union. The Cork union workhouse during the famine, left an indelible mark on the historiography of the city. As an institution the workhouse 'left such bitter memory in the folkmind of the Irish people that one of the first actions of the newly formed Dáil Éireann in 1919, was the abolition of the odious, degrading and foreign workhouse system of poor relief'.[2]

Challenging the role of the workhouse and the effects of the famine posed the question as to whether the physical presence of these buildings on the Irish landscape actually ameliorated the conditions of the starving hordes. Or did they simply contribute to the worst excesses of the famine? Did Cork city ultimately benefit from the workhouse during the years 1845–50? Statistical analyses and a detailed study of the bureaucratic functioning of the house serves to answer these questions.

The workhouse provided refuge for treble its capacity (of 2,000 inmates) and it provided shelter, solace and food for the paupers of the city in addition to its large hinterland. The guardians were at all times consciously aware of the expediency of adhering to poor law regulations but were often moved to assist as many paupers as was humanely possible. However, it was feared that the guardians' humanity could lead to an increased idleness amongst the pauper class if such aid were distributed freely. Economically the commissioners constantly impressed upon the guardians the need for efficient house management and cost consciousness. Amongst the poor law officers especially at higher echelons adherence to policy as strongest. The Cork guardians were willing to attempt both – to assist as many as possible but to also comply with the stringent demands imposed by Dublin.

Recognition of the plight of the Irish pauper in human terms was emphasised in *The Times* (London) in 1848:

> It will be difficult for most of our readers to feel near akin with a class which at best wallows in pig sties and hugs the most brutish degradation. But when we take the sum of the British people the ill fed, ill clothed, ill honoured children of the United Kingdom count with Victoria's own children.[3]

The impact of the famine on Cork workhouse was intense but the guardians were at all times considerate of inmates and their suffering, though at times they appeared to be dispassionate when they refused to challenge the upper echelons of poor law bureaucracy.

Due to the very nature of the remit of being a guardian it is not surprising that the guardians' endeavours were not free of criticism. The city benefited from the presence of the workhouse and without it the death toll would have been much greater. Perhaps the legacy of the building that was Cork workhouse is befitting the memory of those who died. Since those days, it became the county home in 1920, now it is St Finbarr's hospital. It has progressed into a 'well equipped hospital with many departments'.[4] As such St Finbarr's continues the tradition, but greatly augments the care for the aged and infirm, children and adults in it special geriatric, maternity and limb fitting departments. The memory of the impact of the famine in Cork can not be erased but the workhouse should be revered for its legacy as an institution which contributed to the welfare of Cork city rather than the notion of the workhouse as the *death house*.

APPENDIX 1

CORK POOR LAW UNIONS PRE- 1850

1. Bandon
2. Bantry
3. Cork
4. Dunmanway
5. Fermoy
6. Kanturk
7. Kinsale
8. Macroom
9. Mallow
10. Midelton
11. Skibbereen

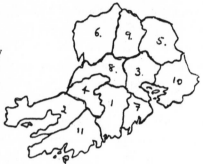

CORK POOR LAW UNIONS POST –1850 (POST FAMINE YEARS)

1. Bandon
2. Bantry
3. Castletown
4. Clonakilty
5. Cork
6. Dunmanway
7. Fermoy
8. Kanturk
9. Kinsale
10. Macroom
11. Mallow
12. Midelton
13. Milford
14. Milstreet
15. Michelstown
16. Skibbereen
17. Skull
18. Youghal

Source: From a map taken from the first inquiry report of the commissioners, into the number and boundaries of the poor law unions and electoral divisions, and subsequently reprinted in Donnelly's *The Land and People of Nineteenth Century Cork*, p. xiv

APPENDIX 2

Questionnaire issued by the editor in 1848 of the Dublin Quarterly Journal *on the recent epidemic fever in Ireland*

The Editor of the *Dublin Quarterly Journal of Medical Science* presents his compliments to Dr _____, and begs to solicit his co-operation in bringing out a collective report on the recent epidemic fever in Ireland. With this view he takes the liberty of submitting to him the accompanying list of queries, to each of which, he need hardly observe, separate replies are not expected. They have been merely drawn up as indicating some subjects on which information is desired by the profession here, and on the continent Etc.,

1. Has the late epidemic fever been prevalent in your neighbourhood?
2. What was the state of health of the district previous to the breaking out of the epidemic?
3. What was the date of commencement of the epidemic?
4. Were those attacked previously in good health or the reverse?
5. What classes in society were chiefly attacked?
6. Did the disease often set in after recovery from the effects of starvation?
7. Did change of diet among people seem to influence the disease?
8. Was the fever frequently preceded by scurvy or purpura?
9. Was there any disease of cattle prevalent at the same time as, or previous to, the epidemic of fever?
10. At what ages were the greatest number attacked?
11. Were males more liable to the disease than females?
12. What was the proportion of cases to the population of the district?
13. Have you evidence as to the disease being contagious?
14. Was there any difference in the symptoms of cases occurring in the different classes of society, and if so what were these differences?
15. What difference in character was there between cases following starvation and others not so circumstanced?

16. At what point did well-marked typhoid symptoms follow starvation state?

17. In what particulars, if any, did this fever differ from former epidemics?

18. Were the purpuric spots common?

19. Was crisis common?

20. What were the most usual critical phenomena?

21. Did dysentery frequently proceed, accompany or follow the fever?

22. What local complications were most frequent and mention their comparative frequency?

23. Did relapses occur frequently?

24. What difference was there between the primary and the relapsed cases?

25. Did petechiae ever appear in relapse, when did they not occur in the primary fever?

26. Please to state any morbid phenomena of the heart which were present?

27. Was epistaxis frequent, at what stage did it generally occur?

28. Was enlargement of the spleen observed in any of the cases, either during or subsequent to the fever?

29. Were bedsores frequent and what was their nature?

30. Was there a greater percentage of mortality among those attended in their homes, or in hospital?

31. What was the proportionate mortality of the various classes attacked?

32. Did the towns and densely populated districts in your neighbourhood exhibit a greater amount of mortality than the thinly populated rural districts?

33. Was there anything remarkable in the post mortem appearances?

34. What was the usual duration of the disease?

35. What was the usual length of convalescence?

36. Was there anything remarkable in those primary cases, which were subsequently followed by relapse?

37. Did you observe any remarkable modification of the symptoms in individuals of the same family placed under the same circumstances?

38. In members of the same family, who had contracted the fever from the same cause, did you observe much diversity of symptoms?

39. What were the usual sequelae of the fever?

40. What treatment did you usually find most serviceable?
41. Were wine and other stimulants used in the treatment of the fever?
42. Was bleeding, local or general, resorted to; if so, please state what was the result, and in what cases employed?
43. Was mercury used; and if so in what cases, and at what stages?
44. Was opium used; and if so, at what time, and in what cases?

Source: Article IV – 'Report upon the recent Epidemic Fever in Ireland' in *The Dublin Quarterly Journal of Medical Science* Vol. VII (Feb. & May), 1849, pp. 64–67

APPENDIX 3

Assisted Emigration

November 1849

Electoral District	No. Emigrants	Cost £	s.	d.
City of Cork	30	112	19	6
Carrigaline	1	3	15	4
Blarney	1	3	15	4
Grenagh	1	3	15	4
Whitechurch	1	3	15	4
Glanmire	1	3	15	4
Union at Large	27	3	15	4

Source: Cork union ledger account book BG 69 CA 7

May 1850

Electoral District	No. Emigrants
City of Cork	200
Carrigaline	1
Carrignavar	2
Rathcooney	1
Riverstown	1
Ballincollig	2
Queenstown	1
Monkstown	2
Union at Large	123

Total Emigration Cost: £825 17s. 2d.
Total Number of Assisted Emigration: 333

Source: Cork union ledger account book BG 69 CA 7

APPENDIX 4

Emigration
Inter-union, Inter-country

Correspondence between the Northwich union and the poor law commissioners in July 1847 indicates an influx of Irish poor into the Northwich union. As evidenced in the letter below, temporary accommodation had to be erected at the workhouse to house those suffering from fever. This preceded the construction of a permanent fever hospital on site.

Northwich, 13th July 1847,

In consequence of the great number of Irish poor who have been flocking into this town and many of whom have been attacked with fever, the guardians of this union not having any other means of accommodating the cases, the lodging house keepers refusing to receive them suit their houses and are in some instances turning parties with fever into the streets, have been obliged to erect a temporary shed of wood in the garden of the workhouse – the urgency of the matter was so great that the guardians were compelled to take this step without first consulting you. However they hope that it will meet with your approval.

Clerk: Thomas Richard Barker,
The poor law court

P.S. You are aware that we have no hospital attached to the workhouse, but I am glad to say that the guardians are now determined to erect one.

Source: Public Records Office, MH12/ 1060, 111126
Obtained from Stephen Penny, curator of the Salt Museum, Cheshire

APPENDIX 5

List of physicians and surgeons in Cork City 1846

Name	Address	
Ahearne, Thomas Mannon	Cook Street	
Armstrong, Charles	Great George's Street	
Austen, Joseph	Cook Street	
Barry, John Milner		
Barry, John William	Grand Parade	
Barry, Patrick		Medical attendant of Cork dispensary
Barter		
Baylie, John		Demonstrator of anatomy in Cork School of Medicine
Beamish, John	South Mall	Senior physician to the fever hospital
Beamish, William	South Terrace	Surgeon to county and city gaols and Bridewell, physician to orphan asylum
Bennett, John	Old St George's Street	
Bull, Christopher	Morrison's Quay	Surgeon in Cork School of Medicine
Bull, Joshua	Blackrock Road	Resident physician and proprietor to Cittadella private lunatic asylum, Blackrock Road.
Bullen, Denis Brennan	Camden Place	Inspector of anatomy for Munster province, surgeon to the North Infirmary and town councillor of St Patrick's Ward.
Caesar, Henry	South Mall	Lecturer at Cork School of Medicine
Callanan, Albert	Morrison's Quay	
Cantillon, Denis	Camden Place	Extra physician to fever hospital

Coppinger, John	Camden Place	Physician to Cork dispensary and lying-in hospital
Cotter, George		
Cuddy, Stephen	Patrick Street	
Curtin, Timothy	Cook Street	Town councillor of Lee ward
Curtis, James	Queen Street	
Daly, Charles	Bridge Street	Physician to fever hospital
Evanson, Henry	Camden Place	Physician to foundling hospital
Finn, Eugene	Patrick Street	Physician to North Infirmary, lecturer to medical school
Fowler, Richard	Warren's Place	Dispensary physician
Gardiner, William Stoker		Apothecary to Cork union workhouse
Grattan, Nicholas	South Mall	Dentist
Gregg, J.		
Gregg, Thomas	South Mall	Demonstrator at Cork Medical School
Haines, Charles	Ballintemple	Attendant at Blackrock dispensary
Harris, Walter	King Street	Physician to Cork protestant orphan society and medical attendant to constabulary
Harrison, Joseph		
Harvey, Joshua	Patrick's Place	Physician to South Infirmary and prof. of medicine at Cork School of Medicine
Hobart, Samuel	South Mall	Surgeon to Cork lunatic asylum, physician to Cork house of relief
Hodnett, Edmond		
Hornbrook, William	Patrick Street	
Howe, George	Bridge Street	
Kehoe, Patrick	Cook Street	Treasurer of Cork school for deaf and dumb
Lambert, Matthew	St Luke's Place	Deputy inspector general of military hospitals

Lloyd, Daniel	Queen Street	Lecturer at Cork School of Medicine
Lucey, Timothy	Tuckey Street	
Lyons, Francis	South Terrace	
Mann, Anthony	Grand Parade	
Mc Evers, John	Charlotte Square	Lecturer and surgeon to Queen Street eye dispensary
Mc Sweeny, Joseph	Sunday's Well	
Meredith, W.		South Infirmary surgeon
Murphy, John	Pope's Quay	
Murphy, Patrick	Old George's Street	
Murphy, William	South Mall	
O'Connor, Denis C.	South Mall	Medical officer at union workhouse and lecturer at Cork School of Medicine
O'Connor, William	Old George's Street	Surgeon and apothecary
O'Flynn, John	Hardwicke Street	Physician to Cork dispensary
Perry, Henry	Grande Parade	
Pickells, William	Sidney Place	Physician to fever hospital
Pitcairn, Sir James	George's Quay	Inspector general for military hospitals, medical officer for Eagle Assurance Co. and governor of South Infirmary
Popham, John	Marlborough Street	Physician to North Infirmary, lecturer on physiology at Cork School of Medicine and medical officer to union workhouse
Power, Thomas	Ballintemple	Physician to Cork lunatic asylum, lecturer at medical school and proprietor of private lunatic asylum at Lindville, Blackrock
Rountree, George		House surgeon at North Infirmary, lecturer of therapy at Cork School of Medicine
Sandham, William	North Main Street	
Sweeny, Daniel	Prince's Street	Lecturer in chemistry

Tanner, William	South Mall	Surgeon South Infirmary and attendant at Douglas lying-in hospital, officer of Scottish Amicable Assurance Co.
Townsend, Edward Richard	Morrison's Quay	Inspector of the county gaol and medical expert for Imperial Insurance Co.
Townsend, William Charles	Old George's Street	
Trayer, Thomas		Resident apothecary of fever hospital
Wall, Thomas		Resident surgeon and apothecary at Cork dispensary
Wherland, James	College Buildings,	Lecturer at Cork School of Medicine
Wood, T.	Patrick Street	
Woodley, Richard	South Terrace	
Wycherly, George		

Adapted from Croly's *Medical Directory for 1846*, pp. 173–177 (Mercer Library, Royal College of Surgeons in Ireland)

Note: *the Physicians most frequently mentioned in the minute books are highlighted in bold print in the above table.*

Cork City fever hospital and house of Recovery, established 1802 under 6th and 7th William IV., cap.116:

Physicians	John S. Beamish (South Mall)
	William Pickells (Sidney Place)
Consulting physician	Charles Daly (Bridge Street)
Extra physician	Daniel Cantillon (Camden Place)
Resident apothecary	Thomas Rogers Trayer

Adapted from data in Croly's *Medical Directory for 1846*, p. 123

APPENDIX 6

Irish workhouses

… there are many things to which all are agreed, respecting the present state of Ireland, amongst those are the poorhouses, their management and support. The management of these houses and the appropriation of the funds levied for their support must undergo a very anfutacy change, otherwise the whole country will be one vast poorhouse. Extinguish, as you will the following … classes: small farmers, grazers, middlemen, agent, nay landed proprietors whilst the profits of the land, the profits of the manufactured article, the profits of trade and commerce … are appropriate to support idleness, so long will Ireland be a pauper nation, or remain an integral part of a great nation, which she will reduce to her own level sooner or later. The question now is … How can this be averted? The paupers in the poorhouse must contribute to support themselves. How can this be done? Whether the sites … do well or ill … for the health of the inmates is not the subject for consideration, they are now built, can they be made available for industrial purposes? They can every one of them and profitably as can be shown by the amount of different professions and callings. We will take up the agricultural department and we hope that some others will take up the manufacturing?

At a recent meeting of the guardians of the Athy union, we find that Mr Cassidy brought forward the following resolution: that the present poorhouses are erected in expensive and ill selected situations, on a very limited quantity of land. We humbly pray that power be given to possess a greater extent of land to enable the guardians employ adult paupers for raising food for themselves

The above resolution is well worthy of serious consideration by the poor law guardians and the rate payers in Ireland. We see no reason why each poorhouse should not have a farm attached to it, sufficiently large to give employment to the able-bodied poor of the union, in raising provisions for the support of the establishment, and teaching its inmates habits of industry. They would then become self supporting establishments instead of being an enormous drain upon the industrious portion of the community or receptacles for demoralising the miserable creatures that inhabit them.

That very many of the poorhouses in Ireland are surrounded by vast tracts of reclaimable land is a question beyond dispute. We will select two out of the many we could name, viz. Cork and Cahirciveen

The poorhouse in Cork is situated on the verge of the unwholesome, death producing bog of Ballyphehane, of little value to the proprietors Messrs Newenham and Copinger, except for the rearing of young cattle during the summer. Why not purchase the bog, sink the river, keep out the tide and drain, reclaim and cultivate it by the paupers and enable them to support themselves? Ballyphehane is capable of producing as good crops of every kind as those grown on similar land by Mrs Evans of Portrane in the county of Dublin. The name of Portrane is now associated with the history of improved agriculture of Europe and aye, America too. Cannot a government with a suitable staff do that which a widow lady did by the aid of one practical Irishman, if this cannot be done then away with your boasted engineering intelligence under government influence, and away with the spirit and patriotic feelings and professions of county and city. If not at our time certainly in a time not far distant Ballyphehane Bog can be made to grow as good flax as any part of Holland and thus giving employment to the widow and orphan. Will the attempt at such improvement be made?

… Ballyphehane Bog contains within itself all the materials for tile making and cheap reclamation …

Almost every poorhouse in Ireland, which facilitates, if taken advantage of, would render such lands highly valuable to the proprietor, who would be secured his rents, to the rate payers, who would be eased of their burdens and, to the country the rendering of such lands more productive and, to society in preserving the mortality of the people and to the state in keeping the entire from being a vast pauper establishment, as it must be if things go on as present.

We find as regards emigration to New South Wales that 'reduced tradesmen and persons resident in the workhouse or the habitual receipt of parish relief are considered eligible for a free passage'.

Such persons must evermore be a burden on society and, nay their offspring must be bred and kept through life as such matters now stand. To obviate this we respectfully call on all guardians of the poor and others interested in the country's prosperity to adopt this course we have suggested.

Extract from the *Farmers' Gazette* in the *Cork Examiner*, 20 Sept. 1847

APPENDIX 7

Thirteenth report of the commissioners of national education in Ireland

Section VI Workhouse Schools

We had in connection with us on 31st December, 1846, ninety-nine workhouse schools, exhibiting an increase of nine within the year, and comprising about three-fourths of the schools belonging to the 130 poor law unions into which Ireland is divided. It has long been felt both by Government and by ourselves that no part of the education of the poor requires of, or admits of, more decided improvement than the instruction of pauper children in workhouse schools. The teachers have hitherto been in most instances been inadequately paid; the consequences of which has been that men of superior qualifications, educated under us are disinclined to undertake an office, in other respects much less attractive than teaching in ordinary schools. In order to remedy, in some degree, this defect, we have resolved with the concurrence of the poor law commissioners, to award annual gratuities to the most deserving of the workhouse teachers, selected by our superintendents. The increase in number of our superintendents with enable us to apply a more vigilant inspection of these schools and we have directed in accordance with the request of the poor law commissioners, that copies of our superintendents reports be periodically transmitted to the guardians, that they may from time to time, be fully apprised with the actual state of their schools. In reference to workhouse schools we take leave to express to your Excellency our conviction, that any system of mere literary instruction pursued by them, would in itself be incomplete in the case of the pauper children, the majority of whom are deprived of the guardianship of their parents. We have, therefore, heard with great satisfaction of the intention of transferring each pupil at the proper stage of advancement to industrial establishments, similar in their general object to the Norwood School in England, in order to qualify them for their different employment in after life.

Source: Cork Examiner, 2 July 1847

APPENDIX 8

Table showing the progressive increase in the national schools, and the number of children in attendance

Date	No. Schools in Operation	No. of Children on the Roll
31st March 1835	1,106	145,521
ditto 1836	1,181	153,707
ditto 1837	1,300	166,929
ditto 1838	1,384	169,584
31st Dec. 1839	1,581	192,971
ditto 1840	1,978	332,560
ditto 1841	2,337	281,849
ditto 1842	2,721	313,792
ditto 1843	2,912	355,320
ditto 1844	3,153	395,550
ditto 1845	3,426	432,844
13 ditto 1846	3,637	456,410

Source: the first report of the commissioners for national education in Ireland, to 31 December 1835–46

APPENDIX 9

Report on cholera by the workhouse physicians in the Minute Book
BG69 A 9

Gentlemen, we regret to have to report that Asiatic Cholera of a very malignant type has made its first appearance in the workhouse. The four first cases were attacked at 7 o'clock this morning of the 9th (April) without any premonitory symptoms and were dead in about eight hours subsequently. The collapse was so immediate in these cases that remedial agents were of littler avail, though used immediately after the attack. Three of these men slept in the same ward which we found to be overcrowded and a fourth in an adjacent ward. They were all country people, and were in a class called able-bodied and were engaged in outdoor labour, exposure to cold and their being unused to the confined air of the workhouse is the only reason we can assign for their being attacked in the first place.

On the same day one case of a milder description occurred on yesterday, nine new cases arose making in all twenty one of whom six have died and four continue in great danger and eleven are nearly convalescent and on this day seven additional cases. The greater numbers of recoveries that are taking g place are in part attributable to the fact that all parties in authority in the house are vigilant in seeking out the cases when first attacked and bringing them to hospital at a period when active remedies are still available to arrest the progress of the malady. From even the short experience of this present malady we feel confident in asserting that cholera is not a very formidable disease when the symptoms are met early and where there previously existed a reasonably good state of health. To attain these objects in the workhouse when the health of the majority is in the lowest condition we have recommended that all inmates should be fed on the same bread as hitherto used in the hospital. That none but the very strongest be put to labour at which they may be exposed to much cold and that all should get their breakfast proceeding to work and some modifications of which we would recommend to all labouring poor.

We have also had a night watchman appointed to go through the wards at night and bring to hospital anyone that he finds affected with the premonitory symptoms of cholera in order that each case may receive immediate attention when first attacked. We have each of us arranged to visit the hospital three times daily, one visit at 8 in the morning and the other at 9 at night; in the intervals, Mr Gardiner will attend the to the cases and send for us when necessary. As cholera has not appeared in the auxiliary workhouse we recommend that as much as possible all communication with the workhouse should cease and accordingly it will be necessary that all cases of ordinary illness or cholera should be treated in that building by a physician appointed for that purpose, during this present emergency, by appointing these measures we hope that the lives of many of those admitted to our joint care may be spared, who would otherwise be sacrificed.

D. C. O'Connor, MD
John Popham, MD
11th April 1849

Medical report on Asiatic cholera in the Minute Book BG69 A9

Gentlemen, since our last report to you of April 25th there have occurred 173 new cases of Asiatic cholera in the union workhouse, viz., 99 males and 74 females and an outbreak of the disease took place on the 18th in the auxiliary workhouse, from which time to the present, 95 persons have been attacked. The type of the disease in the auxiliary workhouse is as yet of a very malignant character running its course with great rapidity. The collapse in many instances being co-incident with the attack, in the upper house we are happy to announce abatement both in numbers and in the severity of the cases.

We have found that a large number of persons suffering from other maladies, have been seized with this disease especially patients who have been for a long time ailing from dysentery or diarrhoea, these cases possess little constitutional vigour to resist a new and virulent disease and too frequently sink at once.

Owing to the suddenness of the outbreak of cholera in the auxiliary workhouse, great difficulty was experienced in making the necessary hospital arrangements but matters are now in a fair train for affording the inmates of that building all medical appliances required for the treatment of the disease.

D. C.O'Connor, MD
John Popham, MD
W. C. Townsend.
2nd May 1849

Gentlemen, since our last report to you, there have occurred 92 new case of cholera in this workhouse viz., 48 males and 44 females, being a decrease of 82 cases when compared to the former week. We trust that we are not too sanguine in concluding from this fact that as the house was the first place in the city where cholera broke out to any extent, so it is the first whereby the favour of the divine providence, some signs of the mitigation of this fearful disease have appeared.

It gives us sincere gratification to be able to state that the results of the last few days are most encouraging as few of the comparatively healthy classes of persons in the workhouse have been attacked, the severity of the disease chiefly fallen on persons who have been debilitated from a course of long protracted illness or other causes pre-disposing them to the attack or any epidemic malady

D. C.O'Connor, MD

J. Popham, MD

9th May 1849

APPENDIX 10

Salary accounts

23 June 1847

Office	£.	s.	d.
Clerk	37	10	0
Master	25	1	1
Asst. Master	1	19	0
Matron	17	10	0
Storekeeper	17	10	0
Physician	25	0	0
Asst. Physician	20	0	0
R.C. Chaplain	28	15	0
Prot. Chaplain	15	0	0
Schoolmaster	7	10	0
Apothecary	27	10	0
Porter	6	5	0
Porter to Board Room	2	2	4

The above table details the salaries of the workhouse staff,
per quarter year

20 December 1848

Office	£.	s.	d.
Clerk	37	10	0
Master	20	0	0
Asst. Master	12	15	0
Matron	12	0	0
Storekeeper	17	10	0
Dr O'Connor	21	5	0
Dr Popham	16	5	0
R.C. Chaplain	28	15	0
Prot. Chaplain	15	0	0
Schoolmaster	7	10	0
Apothecary	27	10	0
Porter	6	5	0
Porter to Board Room	2	2	4

The above table illustrates the changes in salaries (highlighted in **bold**)
for the quarter year, ended Dec. 1848

Source: Cork union ledger account book BG 69 CA 5

NOTES

Introduction

1 McDowell, R. B., 'Ireland on the Eve of the Famine' in Edwards & Williams (eds), *The Great Famine, Studies in Irish History, 1845–50*, (Dublin, 1994), p. 52.

2 *The Illustrated London News*, 4 April 1846 and 31 October 1846.

3 McDowell, R. B., 'Ireland on the Eve of the Famine', p. 52.

4 Devereux, Stephen, *Theories of Famine* (London, 1993), p. 9.

5 Woodham Smith, Cecil, *The Great Hunger, 1845–1849* (London, 1962), p. 63.

6 Arnott, John, *The Investigation into the Condition of the Children in Cork Union Workhouse, with an analysis of the Evidence* (Cork, 1859).

The origins and development of the Cork Union Workhouse, 1838–41.

1 Lewis, Samuel, *Lewis' Cork – A Topographical Dictionary of the Parishes, Towns and Villages of Cork City and County* (London, 1837). This edition with an introduction by Tim Cadogan (Cork, 1998), p. 146.

2 *Ibid.*, p. 178.

3 O'Connor, John, *The Workhouses of Ireland and the Fate of Ireland's Poor* (Dublin,1995), p. 28.

4 *Ibid.*, p. 28.

5 *Ibid.*, p. 34.

6 See map – illustrated section.

7 See map – illustrated section.

8 O'Connor, *The Workhouses of Ireland*, p. 34.

9 First Report of His Majesty's Commissioners for inquiring into the condition of the poorer classes in Ireland, H.C. 1835 [369] Vol. XXXII.

10 McDowell, R. B., 'Ireland on the Eve of the Famine', p. 45.

11 Nicholls, George, Report of George Nicholls on … Poor Laws, Ireland, H.C. 1837 (69), Second report (104), p. xxxviii.

12 *Ibid.*

13 Fifth Annual Report of the Poor Law Commissioners for England and Wales. H.C. 1839, pp. 40–41.

14 Robins, Joseph, *The Miasma – Epidemic and panic in Nineteenth-century Ireland* (Dublin 1995), p. 114.

15 Fifth Annual report, pp. 42.

16 1 & 2 Vic., c. 56 in Foley, Kieran, *The Killarney Poor Law Guardians and The Famine*, 1845–52, MA University College, Dublin, 1987, p. iii.

17 First Report of His Majesty's Commissioners for inquiring into the condition of the poorer classes in Ireland, H.C. 1835 [369] Vol. XXXII, p. ii.

18 Poor Relief Act 1834.

19 Nicholls, Sir George, *History of Irish Poor Laws* (London, 1850), p. 59.

20 Kinealy, C., *This Great Calamity* (Dublin, 1994), p. 158.

21 O'Conaola, T. S., *The Great Famine in Conamara*, MA University College Galway, 1995 p. 107.

22 *Ibid.*, p. 107.

23 Report of the Poor Law Commissioners 1839.

24 Dixon, Hugh, in O' Connor, *Workhouses of Ireland*, p. 78.

25 McDowell, R. B., 'Ireland on the Eve of the Famine', p. 50.

26 Hegarty, Daniel & Hickey, Brian, 'The Famine Graveyard on Carr's Hill Near Cork', *Journal of Cork Historical and Archaeological Society*, Vol. 101 (1996), pp. 9–14.

27 Cork union minute book, BG69 A1, 4 June 1839.

28 *Ibid.*

29 *Ibid.*

30 *Ibid.*, 17 June 1839

31 *Ibid.*

32 *Ibid.*

33 *Ibid.*

34 *Ibid.*, 23 September 1839.

35 *Ibid.*, 29 October 1839.

36 *Ibid.*, 1 November 1839.

37 McDowell, R. B., 'Ireland on the Eve of the Famine', p. 50.

38 Minutes, BG 69 A1, 4 June 1839.

39 *Ibid.*, Letter from the Poor Law Commissioners, 11 June 1839.

40 *Ibid.*, 20 July 1839.

41 McDowell, R. B., 'Ireland on the Eve of the Famine', p. 52.

42 *Ibid.*, p. 51.

43 Sixth Annual Report of the Poor Law Commissioners, p. 30, H.C. 1840 (245), Vol. xvii, p. 430.

44 McDowell, R. B., 'Ireland on the Eve of the Famine', p. 52.

45   Minutes, BG69 A1, 21 November 1839.

46   *Ibid.*

47   *Ibid.*, 12 February 1840.

48   *Ibid.*

49   *Ibid.*

50   *Ibid.*

51   *Ibid.*, 24 February 1840.

52   See map – illustrated section.

53   Minutes, BG 69 AI, letter from commissioners to Cork guardians, Feb. 1840.

54   *Ibid.*

55   See map – illustrated section.

56   Thackeray, William M., *The Works of William Makepeace Thackeray, Vol. XIII, The Irish Sketch Book and Critical Reviews* (London, 1842) p. 82.

57   *Ibid.*, p.86

58   Damp Press Letter Book, BG69 B1, 21 March 1840.

59   Thackeray, *The Irish Sketch Book*, p. 81.

60   *Ibid.*, p. 85.

61   Master's Report to the Commissioners, minutes, BG69 A2, 24 January 1842.

62   Mr Voules' letter, minutes BG69 A2, 12 January 1842.

63   *Ibid.*

64   The lord mayor of Cork, M. Jameson quoted in the *Daily Express* and cited in Appendix p. 3, Arnott, John, *The Investigation into the Condition of the Children in the Cork Workhouse, with an analysis of the evidence* (Cork, 1859)

The role of Cork Union Workhouse during the famine

1   Powell, Malachy, *The Workhouses of Ireland,* paper delivered to the Graduates Club of University College Dublin, 14 February 1964.

2   *The Gardener's Chronicle,* 13 September 1845, in Litton, Helen, *The Irish Famine* (Dublin, 1994), p. 17.

3   Mitchel, John, *The Conquest of Ireland* (Dublin, 1861) in Toibin, Colm & Ferriter, Diarmuid, *The Irish Famine, A Documentary* (New York, 2002) p. 190.

4   John Mitchel was the first person tried under the Treason Felony Act (1848). He spent time in Spike Island, Cork before he was transported to Van Diemen's Land (Tasmania), on board a convict ship

called the *Scourge* in June 1848.

5   Mitchel, John, *The Conquest of Ireland*, p. 190.

6   Toibin, Colm & Ferriter, Diarmuid, *The Irish Famine*, p. 46; Richard Dowden, lord mayor of Cork, 10 October 1845.

7   *Ibid.*, p. 85, William Bishop – extract to Sir Randolph Routh, 5 December 1846.

8   *Ibid.*, p. 128, Joseph Burke, Poor Law Commissioner, 12 November 1846.

9   Cork union minute book, BG 69 A5, letter from Captain Martin to Cork board of guardians, 18 August 1846.

10   Captain Martin's reply to the Cork board of guardians, 28 August 1846.

11   See table 3.

12   Minute book, BG 69 A5, February 1846.

13   Chapter three deals with inmate health, epidemics, fever hospital and medical relief in detail.

14   *Farmers' Gazette*, cited in the *Cork Examiner*, 20 September 1847.

15   Toibin, Colm & Ferriter, Diarmuid, *The Irish Famine*; Joseph Burke, Poor Law Commissioner, letter dated 18 January 1847, p. 129–130.

16   Minutes, BG 69, A9, 11 April 1849.

17   *Ibid.*, 18 April 1849.

18   O'Rourke, Canon John, *The Great Irish Famine* (Dublin, 1989), pp. 243–244.

19   Litton, Helen, *The Irish Famine*, p. 37.

20   Report of the Poor Law Commissioners for 1847.

21   Kinealy, Christine, *This Great Calamity*.

22   Cork union minute book BG 69 A6, November 1846.

23   Hegarty, Daniel & Hickey, Brian 'The Famine Burial Ground on Carr's Hill near Cork', in *Journal of Cork Historical and Archaeological Society*, Vol. 101 (1996), pp. 9–14.

24   Calculated from the Cork union minute book, BG 69, A6.

25   Outgoing letter book, BG 69 B1, 22 February 1848

26   *Ibid.*, 10 May 1848.

Inmate health

1   A transcript of *Famine Year 1847* by Williams, R. D., transcribed by Liam de Roiste in November 1898. Liam de Roiste Papers, U271, at Cork Archives Institute.

2   See Appendix 5 for a list of physicians and surgeons in Cork city for 1846.

3   *Abstract of the Accounts of the Cork Union, for the half year ended 29 September, 1842*, Haliday Collection, Royal Irish Academy.

4   Cork union ledger account books, BG 69 CA5, 23 June 1847.

5   Wilkinson cited in Powell, Malachy (registrar of the apothecaries hall), *The Workhouses of Ireland*, p. 12.

6   *Ibid.*, p. 13.

7   The workhouse referred to is the temporary workhouse (i.e. house of industry).

8   *Southern Reporter*, 23/03/1840.

9   Minute book, BG69 A1, 13 April 1840, pp.159-163.

10   *Ibid.*

11   Minute book, BG69 A5, 21 Feb. 1846.

12   *Ibid.*, March 1846.

13   *Ibid.*, letter received from commissioners 28 March 1846.

14   *Ibid.*, March 1846.

15   *Ibid.*, 1 August 1846.

16   *Ibid.*

17   Minute book, BG69 A6, 3 Oct. 1846.

18   Incoming letter book, BG69 BC3, October 1846

19   Cooke & Scanlon, 'On the Workhouse System', *Evening Echo*, 10/08/1983.

20   Ó Grada, Cormac, 'The Lumper Potato and the Famine' in *History Ireland*, Vol. No. 1, Spring 1993, p. 22.

21   *Ibid.*, p. 23.

22   Minute book, BG69 A5.

23   Jonston, Valerie, *Diets in Workhouses and Prisons, 1835–1895*, D. Phil., Oxford, 1980, p. 13.

24   Minute book, BG69 A 1, March 1841.

25   Northwich Workhouse Dietary, courtesy of Penny, Stephen, curator of the Cheshire Museums Council.

26   Keating, Seán, *Irish Famine Facts*, Teagasc (Dublin, 1996), p. 8.

27   *Ibid.*, p. 11.

28   Lindley, Dr (ed.), *Gardener's Chronicle*, 13 September 1845, cited in Keating's *Irish Famine Facts*, p. 31.

29   *Ibid.*

30   Doherty Papers, Earl of Bandon's Estate Records, 12 October 1846 cited by McCarthy, Patricia, 'Sources for the Study of the Great

Famine held at Cork Archive Institute' in *JCHAS* Vol. 102, 1997, p. 75.

31   Minute book, BG69 A4, 11 October 1845.

32   *Ibid.*, 19 October 1845.

33   *Ibid.*, November 1845.

34   *Ibid.*, 12 April 1846.

35   *Correspondence Explanatory of the Measures adopted by Her Majesty's Government for the Relief of Distress arising from the Failure of the Potato Crop in Ireland*, H.C. 1846 [736] 77.

36   O'Brien, W. P. (formerly poor law and local government inspector, late vice-chairman on general prisons board), *The Great Famine in Ireland and a retrospect of the Fifty Years 1845–95, with a Sketch of the Present Conditions* (London, 1896), pp. 86–87.

37   Evans, E. Estyn, 'Peasant Beliefs in Nineteenth-century Ireland', in Casey & Rhodes (eds), *Views of Irish Peasantry, 1800–1916* (Connecticut, 1977), p. 42.

38   *Ibid.*, p. 43.

39   Minute book, BG69 A5, provisions list for 8 November 1846.

40   *Ibid.*, BG69 A9 and A10.

41   Minute book, BG69 A5, 13 December 1845.

42   *Ibid.*, BG 69 A 11, 3 November 1849.

43   *Ibid.*, BG69 A9 and A10.

44   Cork union ledger account book, BG69 CA6.

45   Minute book, BG 69, A10, 5 May, 1849.

46   Rules governing dietaries according to the General Order of the Poor Law Commissioners, O'Connor, John, *The Workhouses of Ireland and the Fate of Ireland's Poor* (Dublin, 1995), p. 250.

47   Cooke & Scanlon, 'On the Workhouse System'.

48   Minute book, BG69 A6, February 1846.

49   *Southern Reporter*, 25/02/1830 in O'Mahony, Colman, *In the Shadows, Life in Cork, 1750–1930* (Cork, 1997).

50   Popham, Dr John, 'Notes on the Climate and Diseases of the City of Cork', in the *Dublin Medical Journal*, 1853, p. 307.

51   *Ibid.*

52   McArthur 'Medical History of the Famine' in Edwards & Williams, *The Great Famine*, p. 270–271.

53   Robins, J., *The Miasma*, p. 116.

54   *Ibid.*, p. 111.

55   Popham, 'Notes on the Climate', p. 304.

56   Popham, 'Report on the Epidemic Fever in Ireland' in *The Dublin Quarterly Journal of Medical Science*, Vol. VII (1849), p. 80.

57   Source for bacterial information – *Encarta* 1997.

58   Robins, *The Miasma*, p.118.

59   Corrigan, D., *On Famine and Fever as Cause and Effect in Ireland, with observations of Hospital Location and the Dispensation of Outdoor relief of Food and Medicine* (Dublin, 1846), pp.18–19.

60   Popham, 'Notes on the Climate and Diseases of the City of Cork' in *The Dublin Medical Journal*, 1853, p. 306.

61   Geary, Laurence, 'Famine, fever and the Bloody Flux' in Póirtéir, Cathal (ed.), *The Great Irish Famine* (Cork 1995), pp. 75–77.

62   Popham, Popham, 'Appendix to the report on Epidemic Fever in Ireland, Munster Area', in the *Dublin Quarterly Journal of Medical Science*, Vol. VII (1849), pp. 281.

63   Popham, 'Report on the Epidemic Fever in Ireland' in the *Dublin Quarterly Journal of Medical Science*, Vol. VII (1849), p. 82.

64   *Cork Examiner*, 02/07/1847.

65   *Ibid.*, 16/07/1847.

66   Letter from the commissioners to the guardians of the Tullamore Union, in Powell, Malachy, *The Workhouses of Ireland*, p. 13.

67   Bowen, Desmond, *Souperism, Myth or Reality* (Cork, 1970), p. 117.

68   Popham, 'Appendix to the Report on the Epidemic', p. 289.

69   Beecher, Seán, *Day by Day – A Miscellany of Cork History*, 8 November 1848.

70   *Cork Examiner*, 7 December 1847.

71   Appendix 9, report on the cholera outbreak, 11 April 1849.

72   Minute book, BG69 A 9, April 1849.

73   *Ibid.*

74   *Ibid.*

75   See Appendix 9, report to the guardians on the cholera outbreak, 9 May 1849.

76   See Appendix 9, medical report on cholera, 2 May 1849.

77   Minute book, BG 69 A9, 20 March 1849.

78   Appendix 9, medical report on cholera, 2 May 1849.

79   Minute book, BG69 A9, 20 March 1849.

80   *Ibid.*

81   Popham, 'Appendix to the report on Epidemic', p. 282.

82   *Ibid.*, p. 289.

83   Minutes BG69 A4, 30 October 1845.

84   Externs were those admitted and placed directly in the hospital, interns were inmates removed from them house to the hospital.

85   Minute book, BG 69 A5, Feb. 1846.

86   *Ibid.*, 11 April 1846.

87   *Ibid.*, 23 May 1846.

88   *Ibid.*, 30 May 1846.

89   Table is calculated from the weekly returns of patients in the minute books.

90   Cummins, N. M., *Some Chapters of Cork Medical History* (Cork, 1957), p. 105.

91   *Ibid.*

92   Popham, 'Report on the Epidemic'.

The children of the house

1   Driver, Felix, *Power and Pauperism – the Workhouse System, 1883–1884* (Cambridge, 1993). p. 95

2   Figures are calculated from the minute books of Cork union workhouse. Where there are no entries the minute books for that period are missing.

3   Driver, Felix, *Power and Pauperism*, p. 95.

4   Categories were as follows: males fifteen years and under, females fifteen years and under and infants under two years of age.

5   Table is calculated from the minutes available. The minutes in 1851 calculated both boys and girls under fifteen in one category.

6   Letter to poor law commissioners, BG 69 A4, 23 Feb. 1846.

7   28 Feb. 1846, letter to Cork board of guardians, BG 69 A4.

8   Cork union workhouse minute book BG 69 A12.

9   Calculated from the indoor register, BG 65 G5.

10   *Ibid.*

11   Indoor register BG 65 G1.

12   *Ibid.*, BG 65 G5 and G6.

13   Jameson, Mrs, in Arnott's *The Investigation*, p. 40.

14   Arnott, John, *The Investigation*, Appendix, p. 3.

15   For 1845 and 1846 there are complete returns but the minute books for the second half of 1847, all of 1848 and the first two months of 1849 are missing.

16   Arnott, John, *The Investigation*, p. iii.

17   Cork union workhouse minute book BG 69 A5, 14 Feb. 1846.

18   *Ibid.*, BG 69 A5, June 1846.

19   Cork union minute book, BG 69 A 9, 2 May 1849.

20   *Ibid.*, 25 April 1849.

21   Table derived from statistics compiled by Arnott in *The Investigation*, p. iii.

22   Arnott, John, *The Investigation*, Appendix, p. 4.

23   *Ibid.*, p. 41.

24   Minutes, BG69 A5, report of the visiting committee 16 May 1946.

25   Arnott, John, *The Investigation*, p. 41.

26   Póirtéir, Cathal, *Famine Echoes* (Dublin, 1995), p. 130.

27   *Ibid.*, p. 132.

28   Cork union minute book BG 69 A2, 4 April 1842.

29   Minute book BG 69 A5.

30   *Carogue* is the Irish name for a black beetle.

31   Arnott, John, *The Investigation*, p. 30.

32   *Ibid.*, p. 31.

32   Cork union minute book BG 69 A5, 11 July 1846.

34   *Ibid.*, 9 August 1846.

35   *Ibid.*, 1 August 1846.

36   Information sheet containing dietary details courtesy of Mr Collier, curator of the Gressenhall Museum.

37   Cork minute book BG 69 A4, 14 April 1840.

38   *Ibid.*, BG 69 A6.

39   O'Rourke, Canon John, *The Great Irish Famine*, p. 242.

40   *Ibid.*, p. 243.

41   Lalor, Dr Joseph, 'Observations on the Epidemic Dysentery which lately appeared in Kilkenny in 1846', in *The Dublin Quarterly Journal of Medical Science, Vol. III* (1847), pp. 38–56.

42   Popham, Dr John, 'Notes on the Climate'.

43   *Croly's Medical Directory for 1846*, pp. 173–77 (Mercer Library, Royal College of Surgeons in Ireland).

44   Minutes BG69 A4, 17 May 1845.

45   *Ibid.*, BG 69 A5, 31 January 1846.

46   Appendix 7, Thirteenth Report.

47   *Ibid.*

48   *Ibid.*

49   Cork union ledger account book, BG69 CA 5, 23 June 1847.

50   *Ibid.*, 20 December 1848.

51   *Abstract of the Accounts of the Cork Union*, MJ75506.

52   Adapted from O'Connor, John, *The Workhouses of Ireland*, p. 265.

Institutional culture

1   Morash, Chris (ed.), *The Hungry Voice – The Poetry of the Irish Famine* (Dublin, 1989), p. 35.

2   Driver, Felix, abstract to thesis, *The English Bastile; Dimensions of the Workhouse System, 1834–1884*, Ph.D., Cambridge 1988, p. 1.

3   Driver, Felix, *Power and Pauperism*, p. 64.

4   *Ibid.*, p.66

5   Commissioners Workhouse Rules Order 1842, in Driver, *Power and Pauperism*, p. 64.

6   See chapter three.

7   O'Neill, Tomas P., 'The Organisation and Administration of Relief, 1845–52' in Edwards & Williams (eds), *The Great Famine*, p. 209.

8   See also list of misbehaviours in O'Connor, *The Workhouses of Ireland*, p. 108.

9   Litton, Helen, *The Irish Famine*, p. 49–50.

10 Cooke & Scanlon, 'On the Workhouse System', p. 9.

11 *Ibid.*

12 A device designed by Richard Perrott of Cork for grinding corn, introduced into the workhouses to keep inmates occupied simultaneously by rotating a wheel for hours. See O'Connor, John, *The Workhouses of Ireland*, pp. 102–103.

13 O'Connor, *The Workhouses of Ireland*, p. 102.

14 McDowell, in Edwards & Williams (eds), *The Great Famine*, p. 52.

15 Cooke & Scanlon, 'On the Workhouse System', p. 9.

16 Cork union minute book, BG 69 A4 A5 1845–1846.

17 *Ibid.*, 11 October 1845.

18 *Ibid.*, 4 October 1845.

19 *Ibid.*, 18 April 1846.

20 *Ibid.*

21 *Ibid.*

22 Donnelly, J. S., 'Land and People of Nineteenth-century Cork' (Vol. IX), *Studies in Irish History* (London, 1975), p. 89.

23 *Ibid.*, p. 86.

24 McDowell in Edwards & Williams (eds), *The Great Famine*, p. 52.

25 Minute book, BG69 A5, 24 July 1846.

26 *Ibid.*, January 1846.

27 Cork union minute book BG69 A 9, 12 May 1849.

28 See chapter three – Inmate Health.

29 Minute book, BG69 A6, May 1846.

30   *Ibid.*, BG 69 A 9, 12 May 1849.

31   Bolster, Evelyn, A *History of the Diocese of Cork, From the Penal Era to The Famine* (Cork, 1985), p. 314.

32   Minute book, BG69 A1, March to July 1840.

33   Calculated from the salary accounts of 1847, 1848, 1849, 1850 in Cork union ledger accounts, BG69 CA5.

34   Minute book, BG 69 A1, April 1840.

35   *Ibid.*, 4 May 1840.

36   Minute book, BG 69 A3, 10 July 1843.

37   *Ibid.*

38   *Cork Examiner,* 26 May 1847.

39   Minute book, BG69 A5, March 1846.

40   *Ibid.*, 25 November 1845.

41   *Ibid.*, 28 February 1846

42   *Ibid.*, 5, February 1846.

43   Donnelly, J. S., 'Land and People', p. 126.

44   Dowden, Richard, Day Papers 1714–1861, U140 C incoming correspondence.

45   Cork union outgoing letter book, BG 69 B1, 10 May 1848.

46   O'Connor, *The Workhouses of Ireland*, p. 163.

47   Public Records Office, MH12/1060, 111126, obtained from Stephen Penny, curator of the Salt Museum, Cheshire, England.

48   Minute book BG69 A5, February 1846.

49   From the indoor registers 1845 to 1850.

50   *Cork Examiner,* 3 January 1849.

51   Cork union ledger account book BG69 CA 7, November 1849.

52   *Ibid.*, May 1850.

53   Driver, Felix, critique of workhouses in *Power and Pauperism*, p. 67.

CONCLUDING THOUGHTS

1   O'Connor, John, *The Workhouses of Ireland*, Appendix 13, p. 260.

2   *Ibid.*, p. 13.

3   Campbell, S. J., *The Great Irish Famine* (Dublin, 1994), p. 13.

4   Cummins, N. M., *Some Chapters of Cork Medical History*, p. 26.

Bibliography

Manuscript Material

Cork Archives Institute, South Main Street, Cork

Minute Books of the Cork Union Board of Guardians:
    BG 69 A 1 4 June 1839 – 4 Jul. 1841
    BG 69 A 2 19 July 1841 – 27 Feb. 1843
    BG 69 A 3 6 Mar. 1843 – 30 Dec. 1844
    BG 69 A 4 6 Jan. 1844 – 3 Nov. 1845
    BG 69 A 5 10 Nov. 1845 – 24 Aug. 1846
    BG 69 A 6 31 Aug. 1846 - 7 Jul. 1847
    BG 69 A 7 missing
    BG 69 A 8 missing
    BG 69 A 9 21 Mar. 1849 – 16 Jan. 1850
    BG 69 A 10 23 Jan. 1850 – 9 Oct. 1850
    BG 69 A 11 16 Oct. 1850 – 23 Apr. 1851
    BG 69 A 12 30 Apr. 1851 – 19 Nov. 1851
    BG 69 A 13 26 Nov. 1851 – 9 June 1852
    BG 69 A 14 16 Jan. 1852 - 29 Dec. 1852

Cork Union Indoor Workhouse Registers
BG 65 G1: [8 March 184–18 August 1842] this is the first extant register for the Cork union. It lists all inmates, however some personal details relating to inmates are incomplete.

BG 65 G5: [March 1848–July 1850] this register is fragmentary, consisting of the following:
    10/03/1848 – 25/03/48
    16/06/1848 –19/06/48
    21/10/1848
    21/12/1848 – 24/12/48
    27/12/1848 – 16/01/49
    31/01/1849 – 10/03/49
    07/05/1849 – 09/05/49

fragment – no date
17/05/1849 – 21/05/49
22/05/1849 – 23/05/49
20/08/1849
29/08/1849 – 04/09/49
07/06/1850 – 15/06/50
15/07/1850
23/07/1850 – 02/08/50
BG 69 G5 17 Nov. 1850 – 27 June 1852

Cork Union General Ledgers
These general ledgers contain electoral districts, maintenance, establish-
ment, treasurers, provisions, clothing and emigration accounts.
BG 69 CA 5 30 Sept. 1846 – 25 Mar. 1848
BG 69 CA 6 30 Mar. 1848 – 3 Oct. 1849
BG 69 CA 7 10 Oct. 1849 – 25 Mar. 1851

Damp Press Letter Book: containing copy letters written by the clerk of
the Union.
BG 69 B 1 19 June 1839 – 6 Apr.1854

Incoming Letter Book:
BG 69 BC 3 2 January 1845 – 26 December 1846
BG 69 BC 4 2 January 1487 – 31 December 1847
BG 69 BC 5 Missing
BG 69 BC 6 1 January 1849 – 31 December 1849
BG 69 BC 7 27 January 1849 – 31 December 1850

Visiting Committee Report Book: contains hand written accounts of
visits to the workhouse and recommendations of the committee.
BG 69 FM1 8 November 1847 – 19 July 1865

Richard Dowden, Day Papers 1794 – 1861, U140

**Medical Archive, Mercer Library, Royal College of Surgeons in Ire-
land, Mercer Street Lower, Dublin.**

Surgical Society of Ireland, *Council Minute Book 16 Apr. 1831–27 Feb.
1851.*

Butcher, Richard, Surgeon to the Mercer hospital, *Butcher's Casebook 1846–59*.

Kirkpatrick Archive, Royal College of Physicians in Ireland, Kildare Street, Dublin.
The Kirkpatrick Archive contains news-cuttings, etc. about Irish medics all over the world. It includes items relating from the earliest Irish medics to 1954.

PARLIAMENTARY PAPERS

First report of His Majesty's Commissioners for inquiring into the condition of the poorer classes in Ireland, H.C. 1835 [369] Vol. XXXII.

Report of George Nicholls on Poor Laws Ireland, H.C. 1837 [69] 51
Second Report, H.C. 1837 [104] Vol. XXXVIII.
Fifth to thirteenth Annual Reports of the Poor Law Commissioners for England and Wales, 1839–47, Ireland is dealt with under the sub-headings of 'Proceedings in Ireland'.

Correspondence explanatory of the measures adopted by Her Majesty's government for the relief of distress, resulting from the failure of the potato crop in Ireland, H.C. 1846 [736].

Papers relating to the relief of distress and state of the unions and workhouses in Ireland. Seventh Series. 1847–48 [999] Vol LIV.

Papers relating to the relief of distress and state of the unions and workhouses in Ireland. Eighth Series. 1849 [1042] Vol. XLIVIII.

NEWSPAPERS

The Cork Constitution

The Cork Examiner
1845–1850

Famine emigration 13/02/1979 (p. 6)
Cork corporation during the famine 07/08/1978 (p. 6)
Conditions in Cork city during the famine 03/07/1985 (p. 8)
10/07/1985 (p. 8)
Changing marriage patterns in Cork after the great famine 11/08/1978
    (p. 10)

The Southern Reporter

The Illustrated London News
Volumes VII – XII 1845–49

The Evening Echo
Tales of the famine 18/12/1978 (p. 7)
On workhouse systems in Ireland 10/08/1983

The Freeman's Journal

The Fold
Articles on Cork priests during the famine,
January 1986 (p. 11)
February 1986 (p. 12)

The Southern Star
Resume of a talk on the famine in West Cork given by Prof. J. Lee
1 April 1995 (p. 17)

CONTEMPORARY WORKS

Arnott, John, *The Investigation into the Condition of the Children in the Cork Workhouse, with an analysis of the evidence* (Cork, 1859)
Caulfield, Richard, *The Council Book of the Corporation of Cork* (Surrey, 1876)
Corrigan, D. J., MD, *On Famine and Fever as Cause and Effect in Ireland, with observations on Hospital Location and the Dispensation of Outdoor Relief of Food and Medicine* (Dublin, 1846)
Coly & Underwood, 'Diseases of Children', in the *Dublin Quarterly Journal of Medical Science*, Vol. III (1847), pp. 162–165

Croly, Henry, *Croly's Medical Directory for 1846*

Gibson, Rev., *History of Cork – City and County* (Cork 1875)

Hull, Robert, MD, & Madden, William, MD, 'A Few Suggestions on Consumption' in the *Dublin Quarterly Journal of Medical Science*, Vol. IX (1850), pp. 180–185.

Kennedy, George A, MD, MRIA, 'Medical Report of the House of Recovery and Fever Hospital, Cork Street, Dublin from 1 January 1844 to 31 December 184' in the *Dublin Quarterly Journal of Medical Science*, Vol. III (1847), pp. 195–201

Lalor, Joseph, MD, LRCSI (physician to the gaol, lunatic asylum and Kilkenny union workhouse), 'Observations on the Epidemic Dysentery and Diarrhoea which lately appeared in Kilkenny in 1846', in the *Dublin Quarterly Journal of Medical Science*, Vol. III, (1847), pp. 38–56.

'Leboyen's Disinfecting Fluid: Copy of Reports of Dr Southwood Smith, Mr Grainger and Mr Toynbee, and Physicians, Surgeons and others at Dublin. Ordered by the house of commons to be printed, July 1847' in the *Dublin Quarterly Journal of Medical Science*, Vol. IV, (1847), pp. 161–171

Lewis, Samuel, Cork, *A Topographical Dictionary of the Parishes, Towns and Villages of Cork City and County* [first published 1837] (this edition Cork, 1998)

Martineau, Harriet, *Letters From Ireland* (London, 1852)

Milroy & White, 'A Treatise on Plague with Hints on Quarantine' in the *Dublin Quarterly Journal of Medical Science*, Vol. IV (1847), pp. 176–192

'Pathological Reports of the Cork Medical Society for the Session 1849' in the *Dublin Quarterly Journal for Medical Science*, Vol. X (1850), pp. 180–201

Pereira, Jonathan, MD, FRS, 'A treatise on Food and Diet with Observations on the Dietetical Regimen, suited for Disordered States of the Digestive Organs and an Account of the Dietaries of some of the Principal Metropolitan and other Establishments for Paupers, Lunatics, Criminals, Children and the Sick &c.' in the *Dublin Journal of Medical Science*, Vol. XXIV (1844), pp. 479–491

Popham, John, AB, MB, Physician to Cork union workhouse and the North Infirmary Hospital, 'Report on the Epidemic Fever in Ireland' in the *Dublin Quarterly Journal of Medical Science*, Vol. VII (1849), pp. 65–125

Popham, John, AB, MB, 'Appendix to the Fever Report in Munster' in the *Dublin Quarterly Journal of Medical Science* Vol. VIII (1849), pp. 270–289

Popham, John, AB, MB, 'Notes on the Climate and Diseases of the City of Cork', in the *Dublin Medical Journal*, 1853

Thackeray, William Makepeace, *The Irish Sketchbook 1842* (first edition 1842, this ed. 1985)

Tuckey, T. F., *The County and City Remembrancer* (Cork, 1837)

The Irish Medical Directory for the following years: 1839, 1843, 1849, 1852–55.

Abstract of the Accounts of the Cork Union, for the half year ended 29th Sept. 1842, Haliday Collection, Royal Irish Academy

'Report of the Commissioners appointed to take the Census of Ireland for the year 1841' in the *Dublin Journal of Medical Science*, Vol. XXV (1844), pp. 142–145

SECONDARY WORKS

Beecher, Seán, *Day By Day, a Miscellany of Cork History* (Cork, 1992)

Bolster, Evelyn, *A History of the Dioceses of Cork* (3 vols, Cork, 1985)

Bowen, Desmond, *Souperism, Myth or Reality?* (Cork, 1970)

Burke, P., MA, 'The Extent of the Potato Crop in Ireland at the Time of the Famine', in *Statistical and Social Inquiry of Ireland Journal*, Vol. XX (1959–60), pp. 1–35.

Cameron, C. A., *History of the Royal College of Surgeons in Ireland and of the Irish Schools of Medicine* (Dublin, 1886)

Campbell, S. J., *The Great Famine: words and images from the Famine Museum Strokestown Park, County Roscommon* (Dublin, 1994)

Casey, Daniel J. & Rhodes, Robert E. (eds), *Views of The Irish Peasantry 1800–1916* (Connecticut, 1977)

Clifford, Angela, *Poor Law in Ireland* (Belfast, 1983)

Cooke, T. & Scanlon, M., *Guide to the History of Cork* (Cork, 1985)

Cronin, Maura, *Country, Class or Craft, the Politicisation of the Skilled Artisan in Nineteenth-century Cork* (Cork, 1994)

Crowley, Eugene, 'The Development of Cork City' in *The Journal of Cork Historical and Archaeological Society*, Series 2. 48 (1943), pp. 67–81

Cummins, N. Marshall, *Some Chapters of Cork Medical History* (Cork, 1957)

Daly, Mary, *The Famine in Ireland* (Dublin, 1986)

Daly, Mary, *Cork: A City of Crisis, a history of Labour, Conflict & Social Misery* (Cork 1978)

De Breffney, Brian & Mott, George, *The Churches and the Abbeys of Ireland* (London, 1976)

Devereux, S., *Theories of Famine* (London, 1993)

Donnelly, James, *Land and People of 19th Century Cork (Vol. IX) Studies in Irish History* (London, 1975)

Donnelly, Jr, James S., 'The Great Famine: its interpreters, old and new' in *History Ireland*, Vol. 1, No. 3 Autumn (1993), pp. 27–33.

Driver, Felix, *The Workhouse in England, Cambridge Studies in Historical Geography* (Cambridge, 1993)

Dudley Edwards, R. & Williams, T. Desmond (eds), *The Great Famine, Studies in Irish History 1845–52* (new revised edition) (Dublin, 1994)

Eager, Alan R., *A Guide to Irish Bibliographical Material* (Dublin, 1980)

Eriksson, Andres & Ó Grada, Cormac (eds.), *Estate Records of the Irish Famine, a second guide to Famine Archives, 1840–1855* (Dublin, 1995)

Geary, Laurence, 'Famine Fever and the Bloody Flux' in (ed.) Cathal Póirtéir, *The Great Irish Famine* (Cork, 1995), pp. 74–85

Geary, Laurence, 'The Late Disastrous Epidemic, Medical Relief and the Great Famine' in (eds) Monash, Chris and Hayes, Richard, *Fearful Realities, New Perspectives on the Famine* (Dublin, 1996), pp. 49–59.

Goodbody, Rob, *A Suitable Channel – Quaker Relief in the Great Famine* (Dublin, 1995)

Gray, Peter, 'Strokestown Famine Museum' in *History Ireland*, Vol. 2, No. 2 Summer (1994), pp. 5–6.

Hegarty, Daniel & Hickey, Brian, 'The Famine Graveyard on Carr's Hill near Cork' in *The Journal of Cork Historical and Archaeological Society*, Vol 101 (1996), pp. 9–14

Helferty, Seamus & Refausse, Raymond (eds), *Directory of Irish Archives* (Dublin, 1993)

Hickey, Patrick, *A Study of the Peninsulas in West Cork during the Famine* (Cork 2003)

Hollett, David, *Passage to the New World, Packet Ships and Irish Famine Emigrants 1845–1851* (Gwent, 1995)

Hudson, Kenneth & Nicholls, Ann (eds), *The Cambridge Guide to the Historic Places of Britain and Ireland* (Cambridge, 1989)

Keating, John, *Irish Famine Facts* (Dublin, 1996)

Kennedy, Liam, Ell, Paul, Crawford, Margaret, Clarkson, Leslie, *Mapping the Great Irish Famine* (Dublin 1999)

Kinealy, Christine, *This Great Calamity – the Irish Famine, 1845–1855* (Dublin, 1994)

Laxton, Edward, *The Famine Ships, The Irish Exodus to America 1846–1851* (London, 1998)

Lincoln, Colm, *Steps and Steeples of Cork at the Turn of the Century* (Dublin, 1980)

Litton, Helen, *The Irish Famine – an Illustrated History* (Dublin, 1994)

Longmate, Norman, The *Workhouse* (London, 1974)

MacKay, Donald, *Flight From Famine – The Coming of the Irish to Canada* (Toronto 1992)

McCarthy, Patricia, 'Sources for the Study of the Great Famine – held at the Cork Archives Institute' in *The Journal of the Cork Historical and Archaeological Society*, Vol. 102 (1997), pp. 69–78

McNamara, T. F., *The Architecture of Cork 1700–1900*, Yearbook of the Royal Institute of Architects of Ireland (Dublin, 1960)

Miller, Chandra, 'Tumbling into the Fight: Charlotte Grace O'Brien – The Emigrant's Advocate' in *History Ireland*, Vol. 4, No. 4 Winter (1996), pp. 44–47

Morash, Chris (ed.), *The Hungry Voice – the Poetry of the Irish Famine* (Dublin 1989)

O'Brien Gerard, 'The Establishment of the Poor Law Unions in Ireland, 1838–43' in *Irish Historical Studies* Vol. XXIII No. 90 (November 1982) pp. 97–120

O'Brien, W. P. (formerly poor law and local government inspector, late vice-chairman on general prisons board), *The Great Famine, a retrospect of the fifty years 1845–95 with a sketch of the present conditions* (London, 1896)

Ó Canainn, Tomás (ed.) *Songs of Cork* (Cork, 1978)

O'Connor, John, *The Workhouses of Ireland and the Fate of Ireland's Poor* (Dublin, 1995)

O'Day, Alan & Stevenson, John (eds), *Irish Historical Documents Since 1800* (Dublin 1993)

O'Faolain, Seán, *An Irish Journey* (London, 1940)

O'Flanagan, P. & Buttimer, C., *Cork – Historical and Society, Interdisciplinary. Essays on the History of an Irish County* (Dublin, 1993)

Ó Grada, Cormac, *The Great Irish Famine* (Dublin, 1989)

Ó Grada, Cormac, *Black '47 and Beyond* (Princeton, 1999)

Ó Grada, Cormac, 'The Lumper Potato and the Famine' in *History Ireland*, Vol. 1, No. 1, Spring (1993), pp. 22–23

O'Mahony, Colman, *In the Shadows, Life in Cork 1750–1930* (Cork, 1997)

O'Rourke, Canon John, *The Great Irish Famine* (abridged version) (Dublin, 1989)

O'Shea, D. A. (ed.), *Legends, Ballads and Songs of the Lee* (Cork, 1913)

Percy, T. & Kirkpatrick, C. (eds), *Irish Medical Periodicals* (Dublin, 1916)

Pettit, S. F., *This City of Cork* (Cork, 1977)

Powell, Malachy, (registrar of the apothecaries hall of Dublin) 'The Workhouses of Ireland', delivered before the Graduates Club of University College Dublin, 1964.

Robins, J., *The Miasma: Epidemic and Panic in Nineteenth-century Ireland* (Dublin, 1995)

Shannon, Michael Owen (ed.), *A Bibliography on Politics, Planning, Research and Development* (Dublin, 1981)

Snell, D.K. (ed.), *Letters from Ireland During the Famine of 1847 by Alexander Somerville* (Dublin, 1994)

Toibín, Colm & Ferriter, Diarmuid, *The Irish Famine* (New York, 2002)

Woodham Smith, Cecil, *The Great Hunger, Ireland 1845–1849* (London, 1962)

THESES

Cotter, Catherine Mary (Kate), *From Prosperity to Pauperism: the Poor Law Union of Midleton during the Great Famine*, MPhil. University College, Cork. 1999

Driver, Felix, *The English Bastile: dimensions of the workhouse system, 1834–1884*. PhD, Cambridge, 1988 (microfilm)

Foley, K., *The Killarney Poor Law Guardians and the Famine, 1845–52*, MA, University College Dublin, 1987.

Foley, K., *Kerry during the Great Famine, 1845–52*. PhD., University College Dublin, 1997.

Hennessy, Caroline, *The Egmont Estate 1815–1846: with particular reference to the Great Irish Famine*, MA, University College, Cork, 1997.

Johnston, V. J., *Diet in Workhouses and Prisons 1835–1895*. DPhil., Oxford, 1980.

Kinealy, C. A., *The Irish Poor Law, 1838–62: a study of the relationship between the local and central administration*, PhD, Trinity College Dublin, 1983–4

Lindsay, D. & Fitzpatrick, D., *A Guide to Local Archives 1840–1855, Records of the Irish Famine* (Dublin, 1993)

O'Conaola, T. S., *The Great Famine in Conamara: Impact and Assessment.* MA, University College Galway, 1995

WORKHOUSE MUSEUMS

Norfolk Rural Life Museum
Norfolk, England

Gressenhall
Formerly a workhouse, now a rural life museum. Information sheets and bibliographical information were obtained from the curator.

Cheshire Council Museums
Cheshire, England

Northwich Union Workhouse
The curator provided photocopies of archive material relating to diet, nutrition, plans and local maps. Of especial importance was a letter dated July 1847 regarding Irish emigration to the Northwich union.

able-bodied men 43, 63, 72, 75
account books 66, 80, 125, 142, 150, 163
Adelaide Street [see soup kitchens] 47
administration 9-10, 12, 15, 17-19, 21-22, 24-25, 27-29, 34, 67, 72, 78, 95, 97, 99, 118, 127, 131, 135
alcohol abuse 135
alcoholic stimulants 135
amended poor law [see poor law amended] 16
America 141, 157
anthracite 15
apoplectic 82
apothecary 66-67, 153-155, 163
apprenticeships 14, 124
Arnott, John 108-109, 112, 114, 119
arrowroot 88
assisted passage 15, 17, 60, 127
asthma 82-83
Australia 60, 140-141, 143

bacteria 81, 83-86, 89
baker [bakery] 9, 76, 135
Ballincollig 21, 150
Ballinlough 30
Ballyphehane 30, 44, 157
Bandon [see Bandon union, Clancool, Bandon, Earl of] 32-33, 74, 118
Bandon, earl of 74
Banks 17, 22
Barrack Street fever hospital 107
Beaumont, Gustave de 129
Bishopstown ward 21

Black '47 41, 44, 54, 59, 67, 98
Black hole 131
Blackrock ward 21
Blarney 21, 150
blight, potato [phytophthora infestans] 36-37, 52-53, 68, 71, 92, 98, 109
bloodletting 88
Board of guardians 10, 17, 23, 34, 45, 68, 95, 107, 135
Board of superintendents 23, 124
Board of works 72
bog, reclamation of 15
bread, consumption 40, 72, 75-76, 80-81, 89, 118-121
burials [funerals] 51, 80
Burke, Joseph 40, 45
butter 72, 78, 121
buttermilk 72, 84

calcium 80-81
Callanan, Dr 95, 152
Canada, emigration 140-141, 143
Cape of Good Hope 139
carbohydrate 74, 80, 121
carding 11
Carrignavar 21, 106
carogues 119
Carrigaline 21, 150
Catholic 94, 135-138, 163
Catholic clergy 136-137
cemetery 51
cess pools 85, 90-91
Chadwick, wardmaster 135
chamber of horrors 34, 107, 114
children 7, 11, 14-15, 28, 38-39, 63-64, 67, 73, 75, 82, 84-85, 96-111, 114, 116-126, 136,

144-145, 158-159
cholera, Asiatic 48-49, 56, 60-62,
    80-81, 83, 88-92, 95, 106-
    107, 112, 116, 135, 160-162
Church of Ireland 138
Clancool 32-33
clerk of the union 60, 135, 137,
    176
Clifford, Rev. 136-137
coal 15
Cobh 60
Colonial Land and Emigration
    Commission 138
communal washing facilities 121
conjunctivitis 83
consumption 82-83
Convent of Mercy sisters 136
Cook Street 123, 152-153
Corcac-Bascoin 13
Cork Examiner 87-88, 142, 157-
    158
Cork School for Deaf and Dumb
    children 123, 153
Cork School of Medicine 66, 152-
    155
Cork union electoral divisions 17,
    20-21, 146, 150, 176
Corporation, Cork 15
costs [maintainence] 27, 76, 79
County Home 145
Crawford, William 21
crime 34, 107, 129-130, 132-134
crime and punishment 12, 34,
    129-130, 132-133
Crimean war 94
Croly's Medical Dictionary 66, 155
Curtain ward 21

Deane, Karl Allen 22
desertion, children 39, 104-105
desertion, false 39, 57, 101, 104,
    131

desertion, wives 39, 50, 101, 104-
    105
destitution 10, 15, 18-19, 28, 31,
    35-36, 46, 57, 64, 68, 85, 95,
    100-101, 104, 129, 131
deyhydration 89
diarrhoea 86, 88-90, 161
diet [malnutrition, illness,
    nutrition] 32, 65, 71-78, 80,
    86-88, 95, 99-100, 109, 117-
    122, 128, 130, 138, 147
diet [vitamin deficiency] 73, 81,
    83-84, 121-122
discharge figures 31, 47, 52, 57-62,
    64, 97, 104, 115, 132, 135,
    142
discipline 10, 12-13, 16, 29, 31-
    34, 97, 127-128, 133, 135
disease 11, 33, 35, 44, 48, 53-54,
    56, 60-61, 65-67, 71-72, 74-
    75, 80, 82-92, 95, 104, 106-
    107, 109, 112, 114, 116-117,
    119, 121-123, 126, 135, 147-
    148, 160-162
dispensary 16, 152-155
Donnelly, James 134, 140, 146
Douglas 90, 155
Douglas Street 15, 21
Dover's powder 87
Dowden, Richard 68-69, 140
Driver, Felix 98, 128
dropsy, edema 82-84
drstitute rule 18, 35, 73, 120
Dublin 15-17, 24, 26-27, 69-70,
    101, 120, 124, 141, 143-144,
    147, 149, 157
dysentery 53, 82-84, 86-87, 90,
    107, 116, 121, 148, 161

Earle, Richard 16
education 15-16, 64, 98-99, 107,
    123-125, 128, 158-159

Emigration [America] 141

Emigration [assisted passage] 15, 17, 60, 127

Emigration [Australia] 60, 140-141, 143

Emigration [Canada] 140-141, 143

endocarditis 84-85

England 16, 18, 20, 24, 70, 72, 97, 124, 139, 141, 158

English poor law 16, 73, 141

epileptic 82-83

Erysipelas 82-85, 122

Evans, E. Estyn 77

Evergreen Street 29-30

Exchequer Bill Loan Commissioners 27

Expectant mothers 114, 116

fever 36, 44, 48, 52-53, 59, 61, 65, 67, 71, 79, 82-88, 90-95, 103, 107, 109, 111, 119, 121-122, 130, 136, 141, 147-149, 151

Fever act 1846 44, 119-120

fever hospital 44, 48, 79-80, 87-88, 92-94, 107, 141, 151-155

fiscal policies 80, 136

fiscal restraint policies 34, 78-80, 136-137

folk memory 9

Gaol, Cork County 32, 155

Gardeners Chronicle 36

Glanmire 21, 41, 150

Gloucester 141

gout 83-84

Gressenhall 7, 121

Grey, Lord 15

gruel 72, 121

Gulson, Edward 16

Hall, Rev. 137

Hanley, W. 29

Hawley, W. H. T. 16

Hayes, Catherine 116

Hayes, Joseph 21

House of Commons 15-16

House of Industry 15, 21, 23, 27, 29-32, 82, 139, 143

Illinois 140

immune system 71, 85, 112-113, 135

incubation period 117, 123

Indian meal 76-77, 80, 88, 118

Indoor register 82, 84, 97, 99, 103, 106, 117, 121-122

Indoor relief 14-15

infants 68, 85, 100-102, 104, 108-115, 118, 120-122

Kehoe, Dr 123, 153

Lane, Samuel 21

Lee ward 21, 23, 153

Litton, Helen 130

Lunatic asylum 69, 92, 152-154

lying-in hospital 116, 153, 155

Maguire, Fr Augustine 94, 136

marriage, in workhouse 137-138

Martin, Capt. W. 41

Mathew, Fr 51

measles 99

meat 72, 78, 121

medicine 34, 82-83, 95

milk 30, 72, 75, 80-81, 84, 86, 118-121

milk, contaminated 86, 120-121

Mitchel, John 36

mortality 10, 44, 51-53, 55-57, 62, 64, 88, 98, 105, 107-114, 119, 122, 136, 148, 157

Murragh, Henry 24

mustard 89

navy 60
New South Wales 139, 157
Northwich Union 72, 121, 141, 151
nurses 66, 68, 87, 116, 119, 135

Ó Grada, Cormac 71
O'Connor, Dr 66-67, 72, 75, 87, 90, 92-93, 109, 112, 120, 154, 161-163
oatmeal 72, 74-77, 80, 119
ophthalmic disease 82, 84, 121
orphans 38, 63, 97, 103-107, 114, 141, 152-153, 157
outdoor relief 14, 18, 47
outgoing letter book 60, 140

pearle ashes 88
pellagra 73, 83-84
Perrott Richard 131
Perrott wheel 131
Plymouth 141
poor law 9-10, 12-25, 27, 32, 40-41, 46, 54, 60, 64, 68, 70, 72, 76, 78, 95-96, 99-101, 107, 117-118, 120, 124, 127, 130-131, 136-141, 143-145, 151, 156, 158
Poor Law (Ireland) Act 1838 13-14, 16, 26, 72
Poor Law Act of 1601 14
Popham, Dr 66-67, 72, 83, 86-89, 91, 93, 95, 112, 123, 154, 161-163
porter 87-88, 135, 163
potassium 88
potatoes 18, 36-37, 41, 52-53, 58-60, 68, 71-77, 87, 98, 100, 113, 116, 118-119, 121, 130, 133
probationary wards 67
provisions lists 70-71, 89, 135

punishment 12, 34, 129-130, 132-133

Queens College, Cork 66
Queenstown [Cobh] 150

ratepayers 17, 19, 23, 26
Rathconney 21, 150
relapsing fever 83-87, 109, 122
relief charities 47
relief committees 76
reports 15-16, 19, 31-32, 45, 54, 86, 90, 95, 112, 117, 120, 124-125, 134, 147, 149, 158-162
rheumatism 82-83, 85
rickettsia prowazeki 83, 86
Riordan, Seamus 118
Routh, Sir Randolph 76

salaries 22, 66, 70, 125, 135, 137, 163
saltpetre 88
sanitation 39, 44, 48, 57, 65, 70, 85, 122
school 99, 112, 117, 121, 123-125, 135-136
scurvy 73, 83-84, 117, 122, 147
segregation 96, 116, 124, 128, 138
separation 11, 39, 85, 96, 99-100, 124, 128-129, 147
Sheehan, Rev. 136-139
shoemaking 124
sleeping arrandements 65, 121, 123
smallpox 91-92
solitary confinement 132
soup 47, 80, 119, 122
South Mall 66, 152-155
South Terrace 15, 152, 154-155
Southern Reporter 68
spinning 11, 124

St Barr 13
St Finbarr's hospital 9, 145
St Nessan 13
St Nicholas parish 137
staff 7, 12, 30, 48, 54, 65-66, 70, 92, 116-117, 120, 124-126, 129, 132, 134-136, 157, 163
Staphylococcus 83, 85
stealing [theft] 32, 106, 130, 132
Stoker Gardiner, Dr W. 66, 89, 153, 161
Stratford-upon-Avon 140

tailoring 11, 124, 133
teachers 112, 125, 135-136, 163
Thackeray, William 30-31
Townsend, Dr W. C. 66, 88-89, 119, 155, 161
transportation 130
treasury 76
Trevelyan, Sir Charles Edward 76
typhus 52, 83-86, 88, 103, 116, 122

union clothing 32, 106, 132-133

vaccination 91-92
valuation committee 21-23
vibrio cholerae 89
Voules, W. J. 16, 21, 32-34

wardmaster 135
water, contaminated 86, 89-90, 121
Watercourse Road 15
Welsh unions 17
Whately, Archbishop 15-16
Whig government 16
whiskey 87, 89, 135
Wilkinson, George 19-21, 30, 67
wine 87-88, 149
work house [poor house] 9-15, 17-23, 25-36, 38-39, 41-61, 63-72, 74, 76, 79-145, 151, 153-154, 157-158, 160-163
workhouse uniform 32, 67

Xerophthalamia 84

Other Interesting Books

The Great Irish Famine
Edited by Cathal Póirtéir

This is the most wide-ranging series of essays ever published on the Great Irish Famine and will prove of lasting interest to the general reader. Leading historians, economists, geographers – from Ireland, Britain and the United States – have assembled the most up-to-date research from a wide spectrum of disciplines, including medicine, folklore and literature, to give the fullest account yet of the background and consequences of the Famine.

The Legacy of History
for making peace in Ireland
Martin Mansergh

The value of looking back is to understand where we are and why; to honour that which was noble; to acknowledge and try to correct what went wrong. This book helps to flesh out and to put into perspective the background to the problems with which we have had to deal, as well as highlighting what remains to be done.

The Course of Irish History
Edited by T. W. Moody and F. X. Martin

A revised and enlarged version of this classic book provides a rapid short survey, with geographical introduction, of the whole course of Ireland's history. Based on a series of television programmes, it is designed to be both popular and authoritative, concise but comprehensive, highly selective but balanced and fair-minded, critical but constructive and sympathetic. A distinctive feature is its wealth of illustrations.